The Edge of Reason?

The Edge of Reason?

Science and Religion in Modern Society

Edited by Alex Bentley

Continuum International Publishing Group

The Tower Building	80 Maiden Lane
11 York Road	Suite 704
London SE1 7NX	New York NY 10038

www.continuumbooks.com

British Library Cataloguing-in-Publication Data
A catalogue record for this book is available from the British Library.

ISBN: HB: 1847062172
9781847062178

PB: 1847062180
9781847062185

Library of Congress Cataloguing-in-Publication Data
A catalog record for this book is available from the Library of Congress.

Typeset by Newgen Imaging Systems Pvt Ltd, Chennai, India
Printed and bound in Great Britain by MPG Books Ltd, Bodmin, Cornwall

Contents

Contributors

Denis Alexander is the Director of the Faraday Institute for Science and Religion, St Edmund's College, Cambridge, where he is a Fellow. He is also a Senior Affiliated Scientist at The Babraham Institute, where for many years he was Head of the Laboratory of Lymphocyte Signalling and Development. He was previously at the Imperial Cancer Research Fund (now Cancer Research UK), and also worked overseas, latterly at the American University Hospital, Beirut. Dr Alexander is Editor of the journal *Science and Christian Belief* and author of *Rebuilding the Matrix – Science and Faith in the 21st Century* (Oxford: Lion, 2001) and co-author of *Beyond Belief – Science, Faith and Ethical Challenges* (Oxford: Lion, 2004).

Alex Bentley is a Lecturer (Assistant Professor) in Anthropology at the University of Durham, UK. His research includes quantitative models of popular culture evolution (with the AHRC Centre for the Evolution of Cultural Diversity) and the study of prehistoric migration through laboratory analysis of archaeological skeletons. His recent papers on these topics have appeared in *Proceedings of the Royal Society, Current Anthropology* and *Antiquity*.

John Hedley Brooke has been Andreas Idreos Professor of Science and Religion and Director of the Ian Ramsey Centre at Oxford University (1999–2006), and a Distinguished Fellow at the Institute of Advanced Study, the University of Durham (2007). His books include *Science & Religion: Some Historical Perspectives* (Cambridge: Cambridge University Press, 1991), which was awarded the Watson Davis Prize of the History of Science Society, and *Reconstructing Nature: The Engagement of Science & Religion*, with Geoffrey Cantor (Oxford: Oxford University Press, 1998). His latest book, co-edited with Ian Maclean, is *Heterodoxy in Early Modern Science and Religion* (Oxford: Oxford University Press, 2005).

William H. Calvin is a Professor at the University of Washington Medical School, and the author of many popular books on brains, evolution and climate change. His recent books include *A Brain for All Seasons: Human Evolution and Abrupt Climate Change* (University of Chicago Press, 2002), which won a Phi Beta Kappa book prize, and *Global Fever: How to Treat Climate Change* (University Chicago Press, 2008).

Simon Coleman is Professor of Anthropology at the University of Sussex, and editor of the *Journal of the Royal Anthropological Institute*. His interests include the anthropology of religion, with particular interests in globalization, religious language and ritual, and forms of worship mediated through such technology as video and the internet. His books include *The Globalisation of Charismatic Christianity* (Cambridge: Cambridge University Press, 2000) and *The Cultures of Creationism*, edited with Leslie Carlin (Aldershot: Ashgate, 2004).

Mark Hulsether is an Associate Professor in Religious Studies and American Studies at the University of Tennessee, specializing in the interplay between religion, culture and politics in US history. Dr Hulsether's recent book is *Religion, Culture, and Politics in the Twentieth–Century United States* (New York: Columbia University Press, 2007).

Hiroko Kawanami is a Lecturer in the Department of Religious Studies at Lancaster University, UK. Dr. Kawanami has studied international relations and politics in Japan and received her PhD in social anthropology in the UK. She is fluent in Myanmar language and has lived as a Buddhist nun for 16 months in 1986–7. Since then she has been conducting research on the position of Buddhist nuns, monastic education and dissemination of knowledge in Myanmar/Burma, and the relationship between politics and religion in Southeast Asia.

Robert Layton is Professor of Anthropology at the University of Durham, interested in social evolution, indigenous rights and non-Western art. He has worked for Australian Aboriginal communities over the last 30 years. His latest book is *Order and Anarchy: Civil Society, Social Disorder and War* (Cambridge: Cambridge University Press, 2006).

Herbert Maschner is Anthropology Research Professor in the Department of Anthropology and Director of the Center for Archaeology, Materials and Applied Spectroscopy (CAMAS), Idaho State University. His longtime research on the archaeology and ethnohistory of foragers in the Arctic, Northwest Coast, and the Aleutian Islands, has led to multiple theoretical works concerning the evolution of violence and social complexity in human societies.

Mary Midgley was Senior Lecturer in Philosophy at Newcastle University, and for over 50 years has written extensively on religion, science and ethics. Her books include *Beast And Man* (London: Routledge, 1978), *Wickedness* (London: Routledge, 1984), *Evolution as a Religion* (London: Routledge, 1985), *Science as Salvation* (London: Routledge, 1992), *The Ethical Primate* (London: Routledge, 1994), *Science And Poetry* (London: Routledge, 2001), *Myths We Live By* (London: Routledge, 2003) and *Intelligent Design and Other Ideological Problems* (Impact Pamphlet, 2007).

Steven Mithen is Professor of Archaeology and Head of the School of Human and Environmental Sciences, University of Reading, UK. Professor Mithen's research ranges from the origin of our species

2 million years ago to the spread of farming about 6,000 years ago. His books include *Prehistory of the Mind* (London: Thames and Hudson, 1996), *After The Ice: A Global Human History, 20,000–5000 BC* (London: Weidenfeld and Nicolson, 2003) and *The Singing Neanderthals: The Origins of Music, Language, Mind and Body* (London: Weidenfeld and Nicolson, 2005).

Andrew Newberg is an Associate Professor in the Department of Radiology and Psychiatry and Adjunct Assistant Professor in the Department of Religious Studies at the University of Pennsylvania. Board-certified in Internal and Nuclear Medicine, Dr Newberg is also the director and co-founder of the Center for Spirituality and the Mind at the University of Pennsylvania. His books include *Why God Won't Go Away: Brain Science and the Biology of Belief* with Eugene d'Aquili (New York: Random House, 2001) and *Why We Believe What We Believe*, with Mark Waldman (New York: Free Press, 2006)

Michael O'Brien is Professor of Anthropology and Dean of Arts and Science at University of Missouri. For almost 30 years he has focused on integrating evolutionary theory into archaeology, particularly through the detailed analysis of dated artifacts. His scholarly publications, in both biology and archaeology journals, also include work on the history of archaeological theory. His books include *Archaeology as a Process*, with Lee Lyman and Michael Schiffer (Salt Lake City: University of Utah Press, 2005)

Ian Reader is Professor of Japanese Studies at the University of Manchester, UK. His research involves the study of modern religion, especially in Japan, including issues of pilgrimage, media influences, violence and terrorism. His recent books include *Making Pilgrimages: Meaning and Practice in Shikoku* (Honolulu: University of Hawaii Press, 2005).

Katherine Reedy-Maschner is an Assistant Professor of Anthropology at Idaho State University. Her current research concerns fisheries management, indigenous subsistence and commercial economies, cultural and economic development, and traditional ethnography among Alaska Native peoples. She is widely published on the Anthropology of status competition, violence and traditional warfare among Arctic and sub-Arctic peoples.

Michael Shermer is the creator of the Skeptics Society, *Skeptic* magazine, and the Skeptics Distinguished Science Lecture Series at Caltech. He is also a monthly columnist for *Scientific American*, and Adjunct Professor of Economics at Claremont Graduate University. Dr Shermer's books include *How We Believe* (New York: W.H. Freeman, 1999), *Science Friction* (New York: Times Books, 2004), *The Science of Good and Evil* (New York: Times Books, 2004), *The Mind of the Market* (New York: Times Books, 2007) and *Why Darwin Matters: The Case Against Intelligent Design* (New York: Holt, 2007).

Seth Shostak is Senior Astronomer at the SETI Institute, and his research has included studying the dynamics of galaxies and the search for extraterrestrial intelligence. Dr. Shostak is science editor for the Explorer magazine and is the host for the SETI Institute's weekly radio program "Are We Alone?". His books include *sharing the Universe* (Berkely Hills Books, 1998), *Life in the Universe* (with Jeffrey Bennett, Addison-Wesley, 2006) and *Cosmic Company: The Search for Life in the Universe* (with Alex Barnett, Cambridge University Press, 2003). He has published approximately 300 articles on science and technology.

Gordy Slack is a freelance science writer. He has written for *New Scientist*, the *Los Angeles Times*, *Mother Jones*, *WIRED* and *Sierra Magazine*. He regularly writes about culture and science for Salon.com, the online magazine based in San Francisco. His recent books include *Faith in Science*, with W. Mark Richardson (New York: Taylor & Francis, 2007) and *The Battle Over the Meaning of Everything: Evolution, Intelligent Design, and a School Board in Dover, PA* (San Francisco: Jossey–Bass, 2007).

Timothy Taylor is a Reader in Archaeology at the University of Bradford, UK, and Editor-in-Chief of *The Journal of World Prehistory.* Dr Taylor's research focuses on archaeological theory and the later prehistoric societies of central and eastern Europe. His books include *The Prehistory of Sex* (New York: Bantam, 1997) and *The Buried Soul* (London: Fourth Estate, 2002).

David Wilkinson is Principal, St John's College and Lecturer in Theology and Science at the University of Durham, UK. As a Fellow of the Royal Astronomical Society With a PhD in astrophysics, his current work relates Christian theology to the future of the physical universe, and also to pop culture. His books include *Alone in the Universe: The X–Files, Aliens and God* (Downers Grove: IVP, 1997), *The Power of the Force: The Spirituality of the Star Wars Films* (Oxford: Lion, 2000), *A Holiness of the Heart* (Crowborough: Monarch, 2000), *God, Time and Stephen Hawking* (Crowborough: Monarch, 2001) and *Creation* (Downers Grove: IVP, 2002).

David Sloan Wilson is Professor of Biological Sciences and Anthropology at SUNY, Binghamton. His research in applying evolutionary theory human behaviour has led to the development of group selection theory and multi-level selection theory. His books include *Unto Others with Elliot Sober* (Cambridge: Harvard University Press 1999), *Darwin's Cathedral* (Chicago: University of Chicago Press, 2002) and *Evolution for Everyone: How Darwin's Theory Can Change the Way We Think About Our Lives* (New York: Delacorte Press, 2007).

Lewis Wolpert, FRS is Emeritus Professor in Cell and Developmental Biology, University College London. His research interests include the development of the embryo and the evolution of beliefs. His books include *Principles of Development* (Oxford: Oxford University Press, 2007), *Malignant Sadness: The Anatomy of Depression* (London: Faber and Faber, 2001) and *Six Impossible Things Before Breakfast: The Evolutionary Origins of Belief* (London: Faber and Faber, 2006).

Foreword

Can peace be declared?

Mary Midgley

Is there really a sudden new Cold War between science and religion today? Have we somehow lost the very sensible moves towards finding a more rational relation between the two concerns that were made during the last century? Puzzling about this, we might note that many recent converts to fundamentalist Christianity explain their move by saying that they see it as the only alternative to something they call 'Scientific Atheism' or 'Darwinism'. Fundamentalists themselves have, of course, long dealt in this simple, tribal exclusiveness. What has changed today is that they have been lucky enough to find opponents who will confirm this exciting story – opponents who agree that only two extreme positions are open here, and who are willing to give that view a lot of publicity. These new warriors oblige them by flatly opposing 'religion' – religion as such, not just fundamentalism – to something equally monolithic called 'science' or 'Darwinism'. They flatly reject the suggestion that these two concerns, if properly conducted, work in many ways and need not clash because they have different functions – because (as the great evolutionist Dobzhansky put it) science deals in facts and religion in meaning. Such thoughts are now denounced as the reason to the scientific cause. Thus Richard Dawkins writes :

> I do have one thing in common with the Creationists. Like me, but unlike the [Neville] Chamberlain school, they will have no truck with NOMA and its separate magisteria [which was Stephen Jay Gould's proposed formula for separating the two roles.] . . . The teachings of `moderate' religion, though not extremist in themselves, are an open invitation to extremism.[i]

If a number of distinguished scholars were now to denounce Politics, simply as such, on this principle, saying that moderate forms of politics must be avoided because they constitute an open invitation to more extreme ones, their stance might cause some surprise. After all, many things, such as alcohol, are agreed to be harmful in excess but harmless, even beneficial, in moderation. Extremism itself is known to be a distinct and objectionable choice. Yet the current Cold War approach has been accepted without comment by many as rational and proper. Salvoes continue to be loosed in it on both sides. In contrast, the essays in this book suggest that we should stand right back from it and try to understand the confusions that underlie it.

As these authors point out, the normal sense of both terms involved here is a wide one, containing many elements. In order to show them as conflicting, both words must be taken in narrow and peculiar senses. This is usually done by bringing the supposed contestants together in the world of facts, and the chances of history have favoured that move. The tendency of Protestant thought to interpreting the Bible literally, rather than in the symbolic and allegorical way recommended by the early Church Fathers and by much of the Christian tradition, made the shift possible. And the unlucky decision by some American Evangelicals in the late 19th-century to enforce a literal interpretation did indeed ensure a conflict with science.

Thus, campaigning Christian fundamentalism emerged as the guiding myth of a particular population – evangelical Americans, especially the poor and especially those in country districts – who have used it to nourish their self-confidence and have built it into a range of political projects that cause others a good deal of alarm. So it is not surprising if many people today assume, on hearing the word 'religion', that it means primarily this one dangerous thing, fundamentalism, both American and Islamic. (The Islamic kind has, of course, its own political roots, but unless these are understood it too appears as a mysterious, inexplicable menace.)

As these authors point out, however, religion is something much larger than this. It is actually a world-wide phenomenon. Anthropologists think that, in one form or another, it may be a human universal. We cannot grasp its range by reducing it to a single local model, however striking and familiar that model may be. At any point in that range, we need to ask what a particular religion means to the people who actually practise it, and this cannot be done by assuming that all the sentences involved in it should be understood as factual propositions in the natural sciences. When, therefore, Richard Dawkins declares, 'I shall suggest that the existence of God is a scientific hypothesis like any other' (*The God Delusion*, p. 51) he surely displays a startling lack of interest in the workings of language. Sentences claiming that something exists are not even a specially important part of religion. As John Hedley Brooke observes in this book, 'Religions are not just about beliefs, warrantable or not. They are about practices, ranging from prayer and meditation to formalised prescriptions for group and individual behaviour. Christianity has arguably been the exception in being so creedal'.

It surely has, and that obsession with the formulas of the creeds flowed much more from the dissensions of its early days than from anything central to it. A religion is actually a way of life – a distinctive way of living, feeling, acting, thinking, above all perhaps a distinctive way of perceiving and imagining the world as a whole. The speech-patterns it uses are not failed attempts to state scientific facts but responses to how the world as a whole is seen to work. They express background visions, in whose light all particular facts are seen and interpreted. For a believer, God is not an extra item who might or might not be added to the world. He is immanent in it, a feature of its whole nature.

Of course our current culture too has its own visions, which we need to understand much better than we do. But an anthropologist's business, as Simon Coleman points out, is not to defend any one vision against another but to understand them both. From the anthropological angle, what now passes as warfare between science and religion may perhaps be better seen as a clash between the current, exceptionally individualistic outlook of the West and the more communal, less materialistic world-views of other cultures and other times. And in general our first business, when we encounter world-views that seem strange, is not to fight them but to understand them. Indeed, till we do understand them our fighting hardly makes much sense. It is only playing soldiers. So, as Coleman says, 'we need an anthropology, not only of Creationism but of Dawkinsism'.

Robert Layton expands this point by comparing American creationism with a creation-myth of the Australian aborigines, noting that both play important social roles, so that neither can be refuted simply by invoking empirical facts – still less by exchanging insults. And Hiroko Kawanami movingly describes from the inside how this kind of vision can work. She explains the role of Buddhism in Burma, where it operates in the teeth of brutal oppression as the conscience of the nation, constantly directing effort towards the common good. Without any concept of God, the Buddhist origin-myth (fully understood to be a myth) serves to stress the centrality of inner conflict in human life and the consequent disastrousness of egoism, which stops us becoming aware of each other's troubles. That is why serious Buddhists often need to take part in politics not, as is sometimes thought, to aim simply at their own salvation. She remarks, 'It seems to me that, in the post-Enlightenment era, Western rationalists have increasingly privatised religion, and humans have become an end in themselves . . . The weight placed on rationality and science has not improved the human condition, but only enhanced belief in the omnipotence of human reasoning'.

This anthropological approach raises the interesting question, 'Just which science is it that is believed to have finally exploded religion?' Anthropology does not seem anxious to claim that role and, for related reasons (as John Brooke explains), neither does History. The dynamite is, of course, now widely assumed to have come from evolutionary biology, which does succeed in demolishing crude literal interpretations of the Book of Genesis. But that is a very small feat in relation to religion as a whole. And, very interestingly, here we have David Sloan Wilson, himself a distinguished evolutionary biologist and incidentally an atheist, arguing that evolutionary biology itself, properly understood, does not point that way at all, because it suggests that religion is adaptive. The ultra-Darwinist, individualistic strategy that Dawkins relies on to disprove this is an unduly one-sided, and indeed outdated, approach to evolution.

The problem is, of course, how religion can have spread so widely if it is not adaptive in some way. Scholars have usually explained this by suggesting that it promotes survival because it is bond-forming. Dawkins rejects this social explanation because it suggests group-selection – the differential survival of harmonious societies, rather than the one-to-one competition which he takes to be the only real possibility. Besides this, however, he remarks that cultural developments like religion are so large that they need an explanation of their own. This he provides, not (as the rest of us might) by looking at human motivation and surrounding circumstances, but by introducing a quite separate, parallel and metaphysically astonishing process of evolution where immaterial cultural entities ('selfish memes' or genes of culture) compete to infect our minds like parasites and are selected purely for their own advantage, not for that of their victims. Thus a 'human universal' can easily infest our species without doing any kind of good to its members (As Wilson points out, this pattern is closely comparable to demonic possession). Dawkins has since extended the story more widely, but religion was one of his first examples of memetics and its case was surely prominent in his decision to formulate such an idea at all.[ii] He has repeatedly developed similar analogies, for instance in an article called 'Is God A Computer Virus?'.[iii]

Wilson contests both the central doctrines involved here. The veto on group-selection as an explanation of adaptation is, he says, no longer respected by biologists as it was in the 'Age of Individualism' (it is surely no coincidence that it was also the Age of Thatcherism in the UK). Plenty of cases have been found where the harmony of groups clearly has been important in adaptation. And in particular, when we come to a species like our own where communication is highly developed, explanation by factors that promote harmony becomes centrally important. Here, there is no need to wait for the slow spread of a genetic mutation, instead, 'a new cultural mutation can rapidly spread to everyone in the group', deeply affecting its survival.

Has religion, however, in fact played this adaptive role, so that its elements may form 'part of the "social psychology" of the human group-organism'? As Wilson points out, this question calls for empirical legwork, of the kind that is usually expected in the social sciences, about the good or harm actually done – something that Dawkins never attempts. As a first step, Wilson outlines some careful and systematic surveys recently undertaken to compare certain aspects of the lives of believers with non-believers. Of course, as he says, these figures raise as many questions as they answer, but they surely do make a difficulty about Dawkins's sweeping denunciation of the whole province. Enquiries show that 'on average, religious believers are more prosocial than non-believers, feel better about themselves, use their time more constructively, and engage in long-term planning rather than gratifying their impulsive desires. On a moment-by-moment basis they report being more happy, active, sociable, involved and excited.'

Michael Shermer too, cites some statistics which seem relevant. He also is himself an atheist and is seriously worried by many aspects of American religion. Yet, as he notes,

> Religious conservatives donate 30 per cent more money than liberals (even when controlled for income) give more blood and log more volunteer hours. In general, religious people are four times more generous than secularists to all charities, 10per cent more munificent to non-religious charities, and 57 per cent more likely to help a homeless person. Those raised in intact and religious families are more charitable than those who are not . . . [And so on] . . . Before we imagine a world without religion . . . we need to consider what social institutions will be substituted for all the good that religion does.

Clearly more work is needed here, and Wilson is right to call on evolutionary biologists to play their part in it. As he remarks, 'In retrospect it is absurd that evolutionists have spent much more time evaluating the major evolutionary hypotheses for guppy spots than for the elements of religion'. Of course, all attempts to understand our own species do present some special difficulties, but they also have one important advantage which is not available in discussing guppies – namely, they let us do some of the understanding from the inside. They allow us to deal in qualities as well as quantities. We can ask, for instance, just what *sort* of bond-forming is it that particular attitudes make possible? Just which *kind* of happiness is being increased or diminished?

Here we need to note, too, the huge variety among religions. Ian Reader draws attention to this, citing the fable about the six blind men none of whom could see the whole elephant. As Reader remarks, 'Religion is just part of the human realm, as is, for instance, politics. . .. [It] is not an entity that can be isolated as a "germ", held to blame for all manner of ills and then eradicated . . . Religion is morally neutral, reflecting those who shape it; it is neither intrinsically "good" nor "bad" '. The particular form that it takes is up to those who use it.

Science too takes many forms and there is one more department of it which is surely relevant here, namely cosmology. It too, however, is apparently unwilling at present to provide the anti-religious ammunition which the Cold War requires. As David Wilkinson reports, it is now having to look again at questions about cosmic design. 'While the legacy of Darwin demolished the design argument in the minds of biologists, the last four decades of cosmology have seen a revival of the language of design . . . We have discovered that the laws and circumstances of the universe need to be just right in order to give us a Universe of structure and intelligent life'. A whole series of coincidences have been discovered without which, not only would life be impossible but there could be no solid, ordered Universe at all. How has the strange degree of fine-tuning that gives us our present Universe come about? How is it possible for us to be here?

Some scientists now explain this by the 'anthropic' assumption that there is an infinite number of varied universes around us, and the only reason why we find ourselves in this ordered one is because we wouldn't be able to exist in any of the others. This is all right provided that you don't feel the need to reach for your Occam's Razor – that you don't find the enormous, otherwise unsupported invention of all these mysterious universes somewhat extravagant and suspect that perhaps, like memes, they are a product of biased metaphysics rather than physics.

Other cosmologists, like Paul Davies,[iv] think it is more natural to accept that appearances are not deceptive – that our Universe does indeed have some immanent purposive principle working in it to produce the order and activity that we see. This suggestion is not, of course, meant as a proof of the existence of God. What it does is to remove an obstacle to all thinking of this kind – to question the recently-held dogma, actually derived from Cartesian philosophy rather than from science, that there cannot possibly be any purpose outside human life. It leaves space again for religious thinking and more widely, for the awe and reverence with which scientists, as well as other people, have long regarded the physical world – a veneration which is, indeed, surely a necessary part of their reason for doing science. Dawkins calls this attitude 'pantheistic reverence' but insists that, all the same, it has nothing to do with religion. This is surely rather an odd use of language.

What emerges from all these useful forays beyond Cold War thinking? The central point is surely that the Cold Warriors have done us a great service. They have drawn attention to a desperately muddled corner of our conceptual map and their exaggerations show just how badly it needs reshaping. We have long lived with the vague image of two warring provinces, one of which will always provide us with a refuge if the other becomes inconvenient. Our choice between these provinces may largely depend on our upbringing and circumstances – being a known believer can be almost as bad for one's career in Britain now as being a known atheist is in the US. But the trouble lies deeper, in the mistaken opposition itself. We should not need to choose between knives and forks, between walking and breathing. As Einstein said, religion without science is lame, science without religion is blind. Human life is complex, requiring all sorts of approaches and all sorts of tools. We need to be aware of the whole of it.

References

i R. Dawkins, *The God Delusion* (London: Bantam Press, 2006) pp. 67–68 and 306.

ii R. Dawkins, *The Selfish Gene* (Oxford: Oxford University Press, 1976) pp. 205–207.

iii R. Dawkins (1993) 'Is God a computer virus?' in *New Statesman and Society* (18 December 1992–1 January 1993), p. 42.

iv P. Davies, *The Goldilocks Enigma: Why Is The Universe Just Right For Life?* (New York: Penguin Books, 2006).

Introduction

Alex Bentley

Not long ago, I received a group-email from a fellow evolutionary anthropologist, with the subject, 'Read it and weep'. He was forwarding a 2005 report showing that half the population of Britain, a nation with Darwin on its 10-pound note, does not accept the theory of evolution for the origin and development of life.[1] Over a third, in fact, believes in creationism or intelligent design.

As an evolutionary anthropologist, I certainly believe that the Earth is just over 4.5 billion years old, and that we and our culture itself evolve. I worry that some politicians do not believe in evolution. Yet there still seems an academic smugness in implying that our views – which we call 'science' – are more important and any less variable than what much of the population thinks – which we label 'beliefs'. I could see why columnist Michael Bywater[2] would wonder, 'What harm is there in their . . . refusal to play the post-Enlightenment rational game? . . . It doesn't affect the workings of the universe that you are right and I am wrong.'

Does it matter what people believe, and if so, what should they believe?

This is an extremely difficult question. Many of us would favour *freedom* of belief, but we don't want anyone *using* their belief to destroy other beliefs. 'If science is attempting to squash belief,' my colleague says, 'then that is certainly wrong. If belief is attempting to squash science, then that is equally wrong.'

As it happens, however, quite a few on each side would be perfectly happy either to squash religion with science, or to squash science with religion. As Bywater adds, 'the problem arises when they band together to withhold facts from others . . . use their irrationality to harm others . . . or divert resources from more reputable uses.' It certainly is this banding together, as it appears to either side, that intensifies the polemic, but the degree of banding depends on the society. In the US, quite a few (including politicians) are outspoken about their religion. Indeed, the country arguably was founded by people rather insistent about their religion, perhaps leading literally into a cultural 'founder effect' all the way to the present day. In the UK, however, where reserve is culturally more dominant, many follow a philosophy similar to that of country singer Willie Nelson, in that 'your religion is for you, and is best kept close to your heart'.[3] In fact, discovering whether a British person is religious can be a bit like asking whether they have a personality disorder – many would never tell you on first meeting. This may be why the British media were clearly surprised by the prevalence of belief in the 2005 survey. Public perception has it that the UK is a more secular society than the US, yet the UK functions according to many Christian traditions, with its Christian monarchy, a financial year that renews at Easter, chapels integral to colleges at top universities and a longstanding blasphemy law only just repealed in 2008.

It doesn't help that what we see in the public sphere – pundits on television, headlines and media caricatures – often tells us little about the realities underlying society. And many of us rely on our personal experience – we prefer what we practice ourselves – rather than really investigate the complexity of how individual beliefs relate to collective actions. Fear of the Other is clearly a motivator: which is scarier, religious fanaticism or human genetic engineering? The answer depends; not just on our own personal views, as we like to think, but also – perhaps primarily – on what people around us think.[4] Fifty years ago, psychologists such as Solomon Asch and Stanley Milgram demonstrated through controlled experiments how some people will believe other people to the point of administering near-lethal electric shocks to someone, or abandoning their own judgement on questions with obvious answers.

To varying degrees, doing as the Romans do works whether we are scientists, priests, agnostics or zealots. How many Methodists think Methodism is dangerous? How many atheists or agnostics think religion could be important to someone, or benefit a community? How many scientists consider the societal implications of their own results? Objectivity may be easy when reading about exotic religious groups in endangered forests and obscure doomsday cults, but much more difficult in our own. Furthermore, in many of the world's cultures past and present, there is no recognizable religious institution to argue about; religion can be so deeply entwined that it is simply the way people live and how they view their world.[5]

For over a century, cultural anthropologists have peeked into the crannies of the world, seeking exotic cultures and religions. So what makes religious people in our own backyard any different? Perhaps it is because some of them knock on our doors, instead of us knocking on theirs. Perhaps it is a matter of scale and dominance, since a village in highland New Guinea does not have the power or Western arrogance to attempt world domination of thought. Anthropologist Robert Layton grapples with this by asking himself how he could study the cosmology of Australian Aborigines objectively on one hand, but then want to dispute his friend's personal Creationism on the other. Experiencing Creationism in the US, anthropologist Simon Coleman also puts aside what he believes to be factually right or wrong and considers what social purposes Creationism serves for people.

Is religion bad for society?

So what do we *really* know about society and religion? The world of religion is far vaster than our modern experience, stretching back tens (maybe hundreds) of thousands of years across countless societies. Against a very specific few of these – modern monotheistic religions – we have charges of violence, creationism taught in schools[6] and powerful religious interest groups that have shaped politics, laws and even tried to ban movies and books like *Life of Brian* and *Harry Potter*. Arguments that religion is bad for modern society, motivating malicious foreign and domestic events, sell tremendously well in the UK and the US, where many cultural and political roots lie in Christian (but before that, Pagan or animistic) traditions. With books such as *Unweaving the Rainbow, The God Delusion* and *God is not Great*, British authors are doing for English atheism what the Beatles did for

English pop music. From the outside, modern evangelism is seen as a vigorous attempt to brainwash millions into a homogeneous system of thought. To many it evokes the colonial missions of the 18th–20th centuries, which led to the extinction of hundreds of indigenous cultures and thousands of languages.

Within the UK, however, it can be hard to see this resemblance. Christopher Hitchens cites his religious English prep school as foundational in his contempt for the religious, but this is somewhat unexpected now, when Church of England congregations are shrivelling – both in numbers and in skin quality, as the average age increases – and most religious activities are mild and often pleasant. A regular attendee of a small English church might think, what is it about bake sales, Bible discussion groups and mildewed pews that has provoked these attacks? Here in Durham, I enjoyed a certain alertness during a string of Fridays last year, from a church group of youngsters who set up a table on the sidewalk to hand out free coffee in the name of the Lord (as it said on the cup). It was not conditional upon further examination or conversion, just free coffee, a bit rusty presumably for reasons of plumbing, but nonetheless I started bringing my own cup along on Fridays.

In the US, things are carried out on a larger scale, which is why the degrees of euphoria, or alarm, are much higher. When Faith Church, in Mitford, Connecticut, decided to serve coffee, it was not a table on the sidewalk but their own 'SonBucks' coffee house, with Christ depicted amidst their Starbucks-style logo. Coffee is just one of many marketing strategies that anticipate community preferences, and American megachurch leaders tend to use marketing jargon like *branding* and *marketing blitz.* Their use of 'customer' surveys since the 1950s has enabled ministers to 'lower the threshold between the church and the secular world,' as Frances Fitzgerald puts it.[7] 'Seeker' churches grow their congregations by delivering what people want. It is no coincidence that megachurches resemble mega-stores in America, not only in building size, but in the multiplicity of popular services they provide, and the direct relevance they achieve with inspiring messages on daily issues such as marriage, occupations and children.

American megachurches draw in so many thousands that whole towns can sprout around them, particularly in the US South and Southwest. Recalling earlier centuries, megachurches perform many of the civic functions that even recently were covered by secular groups, from girl scouts to bowling teams and the Rotary club. As Robert Putnam discussed in *Bowling Alone*, the decline of these local organizations left a void and a need for community (or 'social capital' as academics call it). By providing childcare, drama and art classes, sports facilities, youth groups and counselling services, megachurches seem good value compared to professional therapists, private dance classes and expensive gym memberships – especially with church donations being flexible or often optional. So although coercion has undoubtedly boosted major religions throughout history, successful religions also draw participants by addressing universal human concerns,[8] the same ones that kin and society have dealt with for hundreds of thousands of years,[9] as Steven Mithen, William Calvin and Lewis Wolpert discuss. Religion serves crucial social functions in non-Western societies as well, as Hiroko Kawanami and Robert Layton discuss.

This is one reason why religion is probably not just a 'meme' as some have characterized it, implying an idea that spreads simply through self-replication.[10] 'It is a stretch to claim that all religions spread through a meme-like process,' writes evolutionary biologist Jerry Coyne in his review of Daniel Dennett's *Breaking the Spell: Religion as a Natural Phenomenon.* 'In practice, memetics becomes an exercise in tautology: all it says, post facto, is that one meme spread at the expense of others because it had more "spreadibility"'.[11] Also, religions have spread, but so have languages, technologies, cultures and people for millennia. These features often spread together as cultural complexes, such as when agriculture, pottery and house styles, and Indo-European languages spread into Europe from the Near East 8000– 5000 BC, or when the technologies, infrastructure and languages of the Roman Empire spread into Europe 5,000 years later. Which bits are doing the spreading, and which ones are hitching a ride? What *causes* one culture to replace or alter another?

Jared Diamond argued that it was 'guns, germs and steel' that enabled agriculture-based state societies to expand at the expense of indigenous communities worldwide.[12] Could a religious meme cause all this in order to spread itself or, conversely, could a religious meme spread *without* its cultural accompaniments? The Mongols, among the most ruthless conquerors in history, were actually quite flexible and synthetic in their religion – open to absorbing new influences. During the 13th-century Mongol reign, Genghis Khan's grandson Möngke Khan told Christian missionaries that the various religions were like the five fingers on each hand, and Kublai Khan even once considered adding Jesus to the Mongol pantheon.[13] Such open incorporation is also partly why Ancient Egyptian gods were involved in everything from storms (Baal) to incense (Dedwen), drinks (Fektet), yearly floods (Hapy), embalming (Anubis), childbirth (Bes), and even snatching and tearing (Pakhet).[14]

Studying how religions arise, persist, succeed and fail among real people requires a complex application of evolutionary theory,[15] rather than the simple, email-like metaphor of memes. Like Darwin and many others, Daniel Dennett has shown how such a simple theory of how things change – specifically through variation, transmission and selection – could be deceptively powerful. In *Darwin's Dangerous Idea*, Dennett marvellously applied it to just about everything, from the evolution of ideas, knowledge and even universes. Culture – which underlies how religions become popular, or how groups behave over time – evolves through ideas and behaviours,[16] which 'mutate' differently and are culturally transmitted and selected in unique ways, so culture evolution does not operate just like genetic evolution (or memes).[17] On this basis, Richard Dawkins' social evolution is critiqued by evolutionary anthropologist David Sloan Wilson, partly based on the difference between Dawkins' *Selfish Gene* model and culture evolution models for how cooperation and altruistic behaviours arise in human groups. Group behaviour is what makes culture evolution complicated, and we are evolved for group behaviour.[18] 'If mirror neuron theorists are right,' says Gordy Slack, 'the advantages of directly understanding others may be so great that they blow the evolutionary costs of occasional self-sacrifice out of the water.'

Should scientists contest religious beliefs?

In early 2008, the National Academy of Sciences and the Institute of Medicine released a short booklet, *Science, Evolution, and Creationism.*[19] Explaining, to as wide an audience as possible, why evolution is science and creationism is not, is a crucial outreach activity that evolutionary scientists should take. The temptation for some, though, is to go a step further. Evolutionists such as Kenneth Miller[20] have rightly taken the 'science' of Creationism to task, but at the same time, Mark Hulsether wonders, have atheists learned enough about religion to comment?

A well-renowned scientist can sell personal metaphysics and creaky social theories through the kind of celebrity 'authority' that he or she laments in religious leadership. Lesser-known social scientists who study religion more intensively may be less trusted, because humans believe more dominant or prestigious people – an evolved innate bias, powerfully reinforced by culture.[21] A recent study showed that we tend to dismiss factual evidence even to believe gossip.[22] Instilled with mirror neurons, as Gordy Slack describes, our brains are actually evolved to copy what is in each other's minds. In my own research, I find copying so prevalent in popular culture that a good model of fashion change simply assumes people copy each other essentially at random.[23]

In university statistics courses, there is often a cautionary tale about identifying cause in some coincidental correlation, like linking a nationwide rise in women's hemlines to the fattening of bicycle tyres. Thus survey results can be notoriously ambiguous; is it *causation* or *correlation* when a survey shows that people express hostility towards a particular country in a place where a certain religion predominates? Arguments like that of Sam Harris confuse correlation with causality,

Mark Hulsether and Ian Reader maintain. 'In the long run, evolutionary psychologists damage their own credibility,' Jerry Coyne concludes (though sympathetic), 'by resting claims about human behaviour and society on flimsy evidence.'[24]

Claiming that a certain belief system (whether atheistic or religious) is 'bad' or 'dangerous' – full stop – is mere stereotyping, possibly an evolved psychological tendency, which we use to make shortcut decisions in the face of too much or too little information.[25] It is no surprise that pundits, religious leaders and even scientists are prone to it. To sell correlation as causation – of which both sides of this debate are guilty – misuses the trust that science must earn through objective testing of multiple hypotheses.

For social scientists, those multiple hypotheses include more direct, economic and political reasons for a downtrodden region to resent a domineering power, as political scientist Robert Pape has argued,[26] which would not go away even if we could 'abolish' religion. Ara Norenzayan, a social psychologist at the University of British Columbia, and his team have studied the practices of thousands of people in various religions around the world. They find little empirical evidence that belief in God – in itself – actually motivates violence. Furthermore, Norenzayan finds no evidence that secularization promotes greater tolerance: if anything, people who believe in God are slightly less likely to scapegoat others and (in Canada, at least) are slightly more generous.[27]

Instead, Norenzayan finds that *dogmatism* is what underlies group intolerance, essentially regardless of what it is about. In this sense, pundits on either side, in their dogmatic faith either in secularization or evangelism as a universal solution, are as embedded into an emotional process. Our own brains are constructed to rally our emotions to protect our personal beliefs when they are challenged, as Andrew Newberg describes. A potential resolution to emotion-charged arguments is objective information, which allows each side to save face by 'necessitating' a change of position due to new evidence. As Newberg reminds us, even expert scientists must filter all facts through a bodily organ – the brain – distinctly variable among individuals, and not at all evolved for objectivity. Newberg can present the same evidence to a group of nuns and a group of atheists, and each happily uses it for their own purposes, that is, for/against a belief in God. Since the evidence cannot be definitive, emotions inevitably fuel the polemic, and religion and politics are notorious for sparking pointless arguments. To many anthropologists and psychologists, the current atheist versus (mainly) Christian 'debate' is nothing more than the age-old Us versus Them battle underlying conflicts from ethnic stereotypes to tribal and national warfare. Pitching one's own 'Us' tent and blaming those outside the tent just creates a dangerously false sense of blamelessness concerning what underlies longstanding conflicts. This too has an evolutionary basis. Violence begins not with a particular ideology about creation, as Herb Maschner and Katherine Reedy-Maschner's Chapter 6 and Robert Layton's *Order and Anarchy* describe, but with our much more basic, instinctive competition over sex, status or group identity. Once the lines are drawn, and the 'Other' is defined, other reasons are brought in to justify the animosity – group affiliations, football teams, sexual orientation, ethnicity, or religious beliefs in gods, behaviours and origins.

The edge of reason

If the debate over the social effects of religion needs more evidence, the debate over the existence of God (or gods, beings or forces, among the varied religions past and present) lacks any evidence at all. In the history of philosophy and science, the issue has never been logically resolvable. It just hasn't, despite all those who have had a try, from Aristotle to Augustine, Aquinas, Darwin, Camus, Calvin, Einstein, Nietzche, Pascal and others whom John Hedley Brooke discusses. Otherworldly intelligence, the topic of Seth Shostak's Chapter 17 as well as most religions, is by definition not falsifiable through evidence from our own world. Just as there is always a number bigger than any number you can name, there is always a possible larger Universe that contains our own Universe, and a possible being more omniscient than our most omniscient being. As physicist Michio Kaku writes in *Parallel Worlds* (referring to quantum physicists Eugene Wigner and John Wheeler):

> If one subscribes to the Wigner interpretation of the Schrodinger cat problem, then we necessarily see the hand of consciousness everywhere. The infinite chain of observers, each one observing the previous observer, ultimately leads to a cosmic observer, perhaps God himself. In this picture, the universe exists because there is a deity to observe it. And if Wheeler's interpretation is correct, then the entire universe is dominated by consciousness and information. In this picture, consciousness is the dominant force that determines the nature of existence.[28]

However valid these theories may be, their scale shows the feebleness in claiming that evidence for biological evolution – which we observe in our world – somehow disproves beliefs concerning otherworldly beings or existences. What could fossil ammonites possibly tell us about such cosmic questions?[29]

As opposed to tautological considerations about the existence of God, we now have exciting new evolutionary sciences of virtual reality[30] and simulated worlds on computers. As in familiar computer games, these models set computer agents within simulated environments, but (unlike games) the agents are programmed to act on their own, so they can learn and evolve by interacting with their environment and with each other. It is entirely conceivable that computer scientists in this century will create a simulation in which the agents evolve enough artificial intelligence to become self-aware. You've seen this in sci-fi movies already, but the self-aware agent needn't be a physical being like the computer HAL in 2001, or the android Data on *Star Trek*. More likely, the agents will feel like the characters in *The Matrix*: existing inside the computer, they will have no way of directly sensing what lies outside their simulated world. What if they ask who created them? If the computer scientists do not intervene, how can these self-aware agents answer their existential questions? As just one thought experiment, imagine that the computer scientists, in their experiment on the origin of religion, seeded the agents with a bit of 'mental' programming containing general clues about their creators' existence.

It may be easier for us to conceive of ourselves as *doing* the simulating than as *being simulated* because, as Newberg points out, our brains are necessarily egocentric. Yet being simulated is just what physicist John Barrow of Cambridge University has proposed, or more specifically, that we might like to *test* whether or not we are part of a simulation.[31] Barrow, who was awarded the Templeton prize in 2006, suggests we look for 'glitches' in the simulation in the way our world works (in *The Matrix*, recall the scene with the black cat rewinding). Of course, any cosmic simulation would have had to set in motion the entire 13.7-billion-year evolution of Universe itself, in which the evolution of life takes place in the latest 3-billion years (at least on Earth; see Seth Shostak's Chapter 17).

According to the anthropic principle, which David Wilkinson discusses, our own Universe is ideally configured not just for life, but for the very physics that make anything possible at all. Logically speaking, there are two possible explanations for existence itself. Either the Universe was created, as Thomas Aquinas (1225–1274) and millennia of religious narratives have maintained, or else ours is just the one of an unfathomable number of universes – the multiverse, as Wilkinson describes – that we happen to inhabit. Before you settle on the latter, however, as being the more responsible, more 'scientific' theory, consider what some physicists have to say about the plausibility of someday creating another Universe by very (very) advanced future technology:

> In our universe, powerful laser beams and particle beams may be used to compress and heat a tiny amount of matter to fantastic energies and temperatures. We would never see the baby universe as it begins to form, since it expands on the 'other side' of the singularity, rather than in our universe . . . But a wormhole would, like an umbilical cord, connect us with the baby universe.[32]

This passage reads almost like a creation myth, and yet it is a plausible scientific scenario.

While the creation of new universes is just theoretical conversation for now, current technologies for genetic engineering, robotics, information technology and nanotechnology are advancing so quickly that radical change will be witnessed in just decades, as humans increasingly engineer their own biology.[33] The potential changes on the horizon – enhancement of bodies, improved mental capacities, extreme longevity – suggest the possible realization of Huxley's *Brave New World*, or new species of humans. As we consider such scenarios, religion would seem increasingly irrelevant for the future, but that is not what is happening. There are not only those retreating *from* science towards religion, but those *embracing* science in a religious way. When futurist Ray Kurzweil says he is 'not planning to die' in Joel Garreau's *Radical Evolution*, and conveys a rapturous anticipation of accelerating human evolution to bring a 'rapid explosion of intelligence and beauty,' Garreau comments that Kurzweil 'is not talking about us someday meeting God. He is talking about us *becoming* God'.[34]

This book is not meant to dwell on such metaphysical questions. It uses them as part of the case that the complex issues of cultural evolution, science and religious belief in society require knowledge of the rich variety of belief systems among the world's societies (anthropology), of religion over the past millennia or longer (archaeology), of what religion does within our minds (biology), of what we do and do not know about the nature and origin of the world (natural science, philosophy, theology), and even the personal opinions of scientists themselves, many of whom are religious.[35] This is the complex, unclaimed territory – the edge of reason – where we stage our debate.

Part I Should scientists challenge religious beliefs in modern society?

1 Science and religion – negotiating the 21st century rapids

Denis R. Alexander

For nearly four decades I have been immersed in the biological research community. As with all biologists, Darwinian evolution provides the framework, the paradigm, within which all our research is carried out. Like most biologists, I do not work on evolution *per se*, instead evolution is the laboratory 'work-horse', the theory that supplies the background for all that we do.

The big theories of science are like amoebae, gobbling up particles of food that then become part of their bodies. For scientific theories, the food particles are the new bits of data flowing out of the world's laboratories. As long as the theory keeps making sense of the data, rendering it coherent, the theory continues to flourish. If cumulative data cannot be fitted comfortably into the theory, then eventually it will collapse or be modified, to be replaced by a better theory.

Darwinian evolution is rare in being a big theory of science that has survived, albeit in a highly modified form, for 150 years. Most really big scientific theories don't survive that long. Like the successful amoeba gobbling up the new bits of data, biological evolution continues to be a stunningly successful theory. Over the past decade, the sequencing of hundreds of genomes of different species, not least our own, has uncovered thousands of 'molecular fossils' that provide a fascinating historical record of our evolutionary past.

One problem with highly successful scientific theories is that their very success lends itself to abuse: the prestige of the theory is used to support ideologies that lie well beyond the ability of science to adjudicate. Darwinian evolution has suffered particularly badly in this regard. Since the publication of Darwin's *Origin of Species* in 1859, evolution has been used in support of capitalism, socialism, communism, racism, atheism and many other 'isms' besides, some of them mutually exclusive. As George Bernard Shaw once remarked: Darwin 'had the luck to please everybody who had an axe to grind'.

Typically, when a big theory in science becomes highly successful, various interest groups move in to try and use it in support of their particular ideology, or the science otherwise becomes popularized with a particular ideological spin. In the public consciousness, the meaning of the label changes, and so 'Theory X' becomes socially transformed into 'Theory Y'.

When Engels was giving Marx's graveside eulogy at London's Highgate cemetery in 1883, he declared that 'Just as Darwin discovered the law of development of organic nature, so Marx discovered the law of development of human history'. Socialists in Britain clearly agreed. 'I am a Socialist because I believe in evolution,' declared the Fabian Annie Besant in a pamphlet of this era. 'What is Socialism,' asked The *Bradford Labour Echo* rhetorically in 1871, 'but the development of a new social organism, where each part works for all, and all for each? It is in the direct line of evolution'. Biological evolution was successfully transformed into early socialist rhetoric, eventually becoming the party-line in all communist countries to the present day. Ironically, Darwin himself was a shrewd capitalist and had no truck with Marxism.

Today the ideological transformations of Darwinism continue in full swing, albeit in different directions. No longer is evolution, for example, just the best explanation for the origins of biological diversity, which as a biologist I take to be the core role of the theory. Instead, it has been ideologically transformed into explanations for almost everything, including a sinister conspiracy theory by scientists to promote atheism.

The contemporary science–religion debate

I think it would be fair to say that academic science–religion studies have undergone a renaissance over the past few decades. When I was a student reading biochemistry at Oxford in the mid-1960s, already with an interest in such things, there were very few books around on the topic. Today there is a plethora of books, conferences, chairs on the subject in major universities, degrees offered, plus research centres such as the Faraday Institute for Science and Religion in Cambridge.[36] An important consequence has been a complete reassessment of historical literature on the relationship between science and religion. Much of the earlier literature, with its roots in the later 19th-century, portrayed a long-term conflict. The more recent literature, which John Hedley Brooke also mentions, gives a more balanced, complex and interesting picture, free of any overarching 'grand narrative'.[37] By 1996, historian Stephen Shapin wrote:

> In the late Victorian period it was common to write about 'the warfare between science and religion' and to presume that these two bodies of culture must always have been in conflict. However, it has been a very long time since these attitudes have been held by historians of science.[38]

But just as the tired old 'conflict model' of science versus religion is finally being killed off in academic circles, the perceived role of religion in world politics, particularly in the US, has again polarized the public debate. The reasons for this polarization are not too difficult to discern. Religion in the US, the country that continues to dominate the world economically, politically, and in science and technology, has continued to boom. The US today is a much more religious society than it was in 1900, by virtually any measure. It is also a very polarized society, in which religion has become thoroughly entangled in emotive issues such as abortion, stem cell therapy and the teaching of creationism and intelligent design in schools.

Partially in response to what they perceive to be the tightening grip of religion on American society, the 'new atheists' have published a series of increasingly robust critiques of religion,[39] often using science as an argument for atheism. The attempt, by Richard Dawkins and others, to invest evolutionary theory with an atheistic agenda is a textbook example of science being ideologically transformed to achieve goals that lie well beyond science. In fact, Dawkins follows faithfully in the footsteps of Thomas Henry Huxley, 'Darwin's bull-dog', who in the late 19th-century used evolution as an ideological battering-ram to acquire for professional scientists – a newly emerging class – the power and prestige of the established church.[40]

As it happens, the clerics of the Anglican Church were quick to baptize Darwinism into Christianity, but Huxley's tilting at windmills proved nonetheless successful in achieving its main social and political goals; even today, the so-called 'conflict model' continues to be well nurtured by the polemic over Darwinism. Young Earth creationists occupy one extreme, denying virtually the whole corpus of current science, and new atheists occupy the other, voicing the view that evolution is somehow incompatible with theistic beliefs. As Simon Coleman also suggests, Dawkins' campaign of atheism may have stimulated the rise of creationism; if you keep telling people who believe in God that 'evolution equals atheism', it should not be surprising that they become attracted to rosier creationist alternatives.

It is no less surprising that publishers are delighted by the polarized debate, because conflict sells, and the media are powerful in sustaining the 'conflict' in the public consciousness. Media give huge amounts of space to creationism, intelligent design and Dawkins, but relatively little space to scientists who argue that their theories should be allowed to do their scientific work, without being loaded with all kinds of extra-scientific baggage.

Negotiating the rapids

The simplistic slogans preferred by the 'new atheists' are useful for propaganda purposes and for political campaigns, but less so for understanding the topic in depth. Philosophers, scientists and historians of science have been active in replacing the 'conflict model' with more complex alternative models for the relationship between science and religion. Amidst a huge academic literature, the Swedish philosopher Mikael Stenmark has surveyed dozens of different nuanced models.[41] Clearly no one single model can possibly do justice to such a complex relationship, either in its historical or in its contemporary aspects.[42] Besides, there is no such thing as 'Religion' or 'Science', only different religions and different scientific disciplines, which of course vary hugely in different historical era.

One in particular that I find useful is the model of 'integrated complementarity' (see Figure 1). The levels of explanation are modelled as slices of a cube, representing the sum of all we experience – the book of life, if you like. In reality it is one cube, one book, but our brains are simply not Herculean enough to grasp it all at one go. The scientific level of understanding tells us how things work and where they come from; the moral and ethical level addresses what we *ought* to do in the world; the aesthetic level concerns our understanding and appreciation of beauty; and the personal level addresses our biographies in the world. And so forth – you can add levels according to taste. At the religious level, the relevant type of questions to ask are 'Why is there a universe anyway?', 'What breathes fire into the equations?', 'Does life have any purpose in an ultimate sense?' and 'Does God exist?'.

These various explanatory levels of the Model are not rivals, but rather complementary explanations – we need them all to do justice to our own experience as human agents. Each explanatory level has its own particular means of justification – historians have their ways, lawyers, molecular biologists, theologians and anthropologists each has his or her way, as other chapters of this book will show. Only 'greedy reductionists', to use Daniel Dennet's phrase, will try and

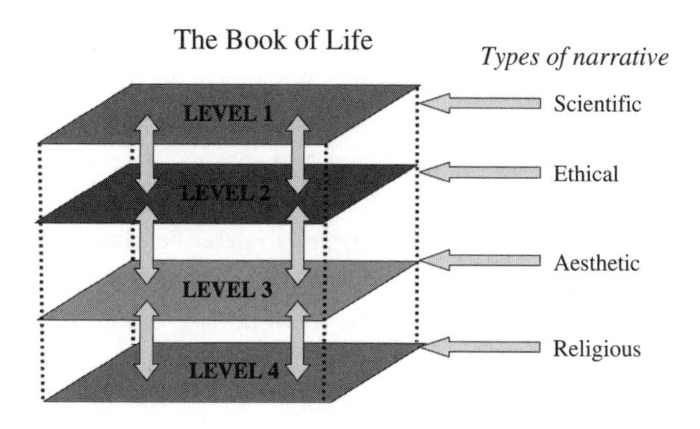

Figure 1 Complementary narratives are necessary to explain the complex reality of life.

reduce all valid knowledge to their particular explanatory level. In fact, the Model reflects the structure of universities, where different forms of enquiry coexist with each other, ideally while appreciating different ways of acquiring well-justified beliefs.

The danger in such a Model is that the different explanatory narratives come to be seen in glorious isolation. In Stephen Jay Gould's so-called 'Non-Overlapping Magisteria', science and religion are maintained in well-separated compartments.[43] But the constant traffic of ideas between science and religion, over the centuries to the present day, does not indicate separate realms for these human activities. The vertical arrows between the different explanatory levels (see Figure 1) are indeed important, fascinating areas of enquiry.

Most scientists are practising complementarians, even if they do not use that precise language. No one really believes that science has all the answers to *all* questions. No one (in their right mind) actually behaves as if science is all we need. 'The pre-eminent mystery is why anything exists at all,' Lord Martin Rees, President of the Royal Society, has commented, 'What breathes life into the equations, and actualized them in a real cosmos? Such questions lie beyond science . . . they are the province of philosophers and theologians'. That is a common view among scientists.

So how would we apply the integrated complementarity model to the relationship between, for example, the Christian doctrine of creation and Darwinian evolution? The Christian doctrine of creation is not mainly about origins as is commonly imagined, but rather about the purported dependence of everything that exists upon the creative will of God, including past, present and future. The only one great dualism in Christian theology lies between God and everything else that exists. In this view, therefore, scientists describe what God does to the best of their ability. As Augustine put it in the early 5th century, 'Nature is what God does'.[44] The evolutionary account therefore provides the scientific description of how God has brought biological diversity into being. The scientific and theological narratives are complementary. Putting it crudely, the scientific account describes how it happened, the theological account why it happened.

This robust theism represents belief in a God who is intimately involved, immanent in the created order and no absentee landlord. It helps to explain how Darwinism was baptized into a Christian world-view so soon after 1859. Enthusiasts for Darwin within the Anglican Church in England, such as Kingsley, Temple and Moore, saw evolution as usefully countering the deistic implications of natural theology. 'Darwinism appeared, and, under the guise of a foe, did the work of a friend' wrote Aubrey Moore, Fellow of St. John's College and Curator of the Oxford Botanical Gardens. Amid a huge range of responses to the *Origin of Species*, the theological resources were already available to absorb the new theory into Christian faith. Reading the 19th-century literature does make one acutely aware how theologically distant is the Young Earth Creationism that came to prominence in the late 20th-century.

Of course, evolution can be readily absorbed into virtually any metaphysical or religious world-view imaginable, such as the Abrahamic faiths, Buddhism, Hinduism or Atheism. The reasons are not hard to see, if you perceive Darwinism as scientists perceive it, as a brilliant explanation for the origins of biological diversity. Evolutionary theory itself simply cannot adjudicate between rival metaphysical beliefs, any more than can other scientific theories. People will always bring their prior metaphysical beliefs to the science and encompass their science within that particular world-view. When conflict arises in science–religion interactions, it is frequently because one stake-holder or another seeks either to invest science with an ideological load that it was never designed to bear, or to claim religious beliefs can decide what is quite clearly a question for science.

Should scientists contest religious beliefs in modern society? My answer involves four assertions.

First, scientists should stick to what they are good at. Personal ideologies lie well beyond science. Pontificating in the public domain on matters outside their area of expertise damages science education as well as public understanding, as the public then respond to the socially transformed 'Theory Y' rather than to the actual scientific 'Theory X'. Campaigns to invest evolution with ideological baggage are not good for science education.

Second, it is clearly within the remit of scientists to speak into the public domain to correct factual errors. The Earth is not 10,000 years old. Antibiotics are of no use against viral infections. Blood transfusions can save your life. Having sex with a young female virgin will not protect you from HIV. And so forth. If the current science contradicts some religious belief or other, then a robust religion should be able to cope. On no account should the religion be allowed to censor the science.

Third, science education should be reserved for science, without the extra-scientific questions, for which the list is endless. I don't talk about the politics of AIDS in Africa when giving my Part 2 immunology lectures at Cambridge. Even though the topic is of critical importance, it isn't appropriate in lectures on molecular immunology. If I were teaching international health sciences it would be different. Likewise, neither creationism nor intelligent design should be taught in science classrooms, because they are not scientific theories and do not feature at all in current biology. A science curriculum should convey the current understanding of scientific theories as discussed by the scientific community, for which neither creationism nor intelligent design qualifies.

Fourth, all the non-science topics are fair game for religious studies, civilization or philosophy classes. There is a growing corpus of useful websites and print materials for resourcing the teaching of science and religion in schools in an engaging, informed and balanced manner.[45] The Faraday Institute organizes short courses by top speakers in the field, open to any undergraduate or graduate from any university in the world.[46] I have some hope that the media might start reporting the science–religion arena in a rather more educated and less polarized way. For example, every summer, courses are held in Cambridge at which selected high-profile media personnel are given a broad education in the science–religion debate, and there is good evidence that this is feeding through into some more educated reporting on the subject.[47]

Plenty of resources are available for negotiating the rapids in the current science–religion debate. If we can wean people off the polarized sloganeering, and encourage thoughtful and well-informed dialogue, then I see a lot of hope for the future of science–faith interactions.

2 Why new atheist definitions of religions fail

Mark Hulsether

Suppose I want to criticize a group that exhibits behaviour X. If I can show that X is unacceptable, have I proved my case? We could imagine situations in which this would follow. For example, suppose the group in question is a set of computer viruses that share the behaviour of destroying all data on computers where they are introduced. We could easily show that this is unacceptable, and it would follow that the group is unacceptable; we might even consider making it illegal to promote this group via email, notwithstanding the right of free speech and the virtue of liberal toleration. If X is a virus, a group defined by X has little to recommend it.

However, suppose another set of people has long understood itself as Group W and has been described as such by others. Some members of this group exhibit an unacceptable behaviour X, but other members exhibit virtue A, which is an effort to stamp out X. People in the group also exhibit many more behaviours, including several that outsiders consider beneficial and some that outsiders do not care about one way or the other, but which make group members happy. In fact the group exhibits dozens of behaviours, A through X. Most members exhibit many of them but not a single member exhibits all of them. The group is what scholars call a 'fuzzy set' – it is based on family resemblances and shared patterns. Several of its traits (including the conflict over X) are sources of internal disagreement.[48]

This is roughly the situation that confronts new atheists, such as Sam Harris, when they criticize religion.[49] For Group W in our thought experiment we can substitute religious traditions, for critiques of X we can substitute Harris's rationalist arguments that debunk selected religious beliefs, and for the fuzziness of our group we can substitute the complexity of religions as they actually exist. Before turning to these matters, let us pursue our thought experiment one step further.

Suppose I make a strong case that behaviour X (as practised in Group W) is unacceptable. What would follow? Have I won the right to make sweeping attacks on the entire group – including a group member named Martha who engages in behaviour A but not X? Suppose I emphasize that my argument does not pussyfoot around with humanistic fuzzy sets; it *defines* Group W as *constituted* by those who exhibit behaviour X. Thus, I claim that Martha is unjustified when she objects to my approach; she is introducing confusion into my clean scientific argument and exhibiting the irrational emotionalism that I have come to expect from her kind. Suppose I insist that she must dissociate herself from Group W, because (although she claims to practice A) any rational person can see that she is enabling X. She must move outside Group W in order to combat X, because I have identified this group with rational precision as people who practice X. It is too much trouble to explore all the group's messy traits from A through X – traits that work in layers, continually evolve, and fight with each other. It is enough to show that X pollutes some of these layers.

Such is the logic of new atheists. For Harris and others of his ilk, the core X trait, to which they return over and over, is irrational belief in false propositions about supernatural beings.[50] By extension it includes teachings (especially from the Bible and Qur'an) said to be commanded by such beings. Religion is seen to be mainly about conceptual propositions, and these propositions refer to gods that do not exist.

Recall how I instructed Martha that she is not really part of Group W, despite what she has thought for years. This is how Harris addresses religious people who are open minded and anti-authoritarian. In his *Letter to a Christian Nation* he grants that 'moderate Christians will not always recognize themselves' in his arguments, primarily because they claim the existence of a 'terrain between atheism and fundamentalism.'[51] However, by his fifth page he delimits his attention to 'Christianity in its most committed forms' and 'the narrow sense.' These are Christians who agree with him on what he takes as core issues: 'if the basic tenets of Christianity are true' he will go to hell, and 'one side is really going to win this argument and the other side is really going to lose.'[52] Harris knows what defines members of Martha's group better than she does. Huge numbers, probably a majority, of US Christians do not take the Bible literally. Yet Harris assures us that 'if a Christian made no tacit claims of knowledge with regard to the literal truth of scripture,' then such a person 'would be just as much a Muslim, or a Jew – or an atheist – as a follower of Christ.' Religious moderates 'relax [their] standards of adherence to ancient superstitions and taboos, while otherwise maintaining a belief system' based on ignorance. They 'betray faith and reason equally' and must choose sides.[53]

One possible response to this argument is to politely ignore it.[54] A colleague with long experience in religious studies commented that new atheists 'do not seem to have a clue as to what it might be like to live, worship, doubt, resist, critique, give thanks, consider the lilies, marvel at the handiwork of Creation, stay with the weaker brethren, forgive, etc., inside a company of faithful people.' He judged that Richard Dawkins is 'ignored by leading theologians and philosophers of religion primarily because he seems so tiresomely and doggedly to remain at the Freshman Introductory Course level.' (Even introductory religious studies courses, however, stress that conceptual belief is only one dimension of religion among others, that conventional Christian ideas about the supernatural are just one approach to belief, and that a minimal requirement for studying the world's religions is thinking comparatively about many forms of religious life.) Boiling down this sort of critique more pungently, another colleague recalled his response to a friend who tried to debunk his religious ideas: 'You don't know enough about religion to be an atheist!'[55]

However, even if we agree that new atheists have little clue about life in existing religious groups, it is harder to agree that all leading scholars of religion have ignored them. In this regard it matters which scholarly conversations we follow, because new atheists are not only influential in popular culture; some of their ideas have gained substantial momentum in the academic study of religion. Although kindred scholars evade Harris's most egregious oversimplifications, there is often overlap in key trains of thought.[56]

New atheists may protest that I have not presented their case at its strongest. The point is not, they may object, that they fail to grasp how religious life includes multiple layers. Rather, they have lost patience with anyone who denies a need to discern which of these layers deserve priority, especially for definitions that are focused enough to be useful. A discerning observer, they claim, can see that behaviour X is the crucial layer and that X pollutes the other layers. At this juncture Harris could strengthen his argument if he proceeded less rigidly and more contextually. He could grant that irrational belief in non-existent gods does not describe all layers of all religions, while showing how it characterizes major layers of important religions. He could bring his analysis down to cases and show that in certain times and places the key forms of religion are vulnerable to his attack.

Unfortunately he does not proceed contextually, and he wildly overreaches insofar as he expects us to take his critiques seriously as universal claims. Does Harris know enough about religion to be an atheist? Is it true that irrational conceptual propositions about gods are the most important characteristic of religion? Who has the right to say? No doubt we need focused analyses informed by clear working definitions of religion; some fuzzy set approaches have been so wide open that religion winds up meaning pretty much anything a scholar wishes, and for this reason nothing much in particular. Still the question remains, who decides when a definition is too broad to be useful, or too narrow – or, more pointedly, when the definition is acceptable despite defining all religion as false, all seekers of true ideas as unreligious, and most working academic theologians as irrelevant to religion? If a religious group is too complex for single-factor definitions, then both scholars and group members (who may be the same people) should object. We can easily agree that religions may foster irrational and dangerous ideas, and that religious leaders have no right to control scholarly discussions – but are they disqualified to speak in such discussions at all, even in scholarly ways? Are they excluded by definition?

Let us relate these questions to a concrete case. In her song 'I See Who You Are,' the musician Björk calls on two lovers to 'celebrate now all this flesh on our bones,' because 'later this century . . . you and I [will] become corpses.' She imagines a lover who can 'see who you are behind the skin and muscles,' and she evokes powerful and elusive registers of meaning through sound.[57] Now, the important thing about this song is that it articulates insights about life which are worth cultivating; this matters more than whether we categorize the song as religious, spiritual but not religious, or neither religious nor spiritual. Nevertheless, it is worth noting that Harris would see Björk's insights as the *opposite* of a religious sensibility. Along with blunt assertions such as 'religion is nothing more than bad concepts held in place of good ones for all time,' he argues that religions devalue material life and substitute visions of the afterlife.[58] Thus he compiles a gruesome list of examples of blood sacrifice, building to a conclusion that 'astride this contemptible history of religious atrocity and scientific ignorance, Christianity now stands as an absurdly unselfconscious apotheosis.'[59] He claims that 'once you stop swaddling the reality of the world's suffering in religious fantasies, you will feel in your bones just how precious life is.'[60] To 'celebrate now all this flesh on our bones' is to capture much of what Harris sees as the antithesis of a religious mode of being.

Meanwhile, I perceive Björk articulating powerful spiritual/religious insights. I understand religions/spiritualities as forms of language/behaviour through which one can express and cultivate valuable insights about life – or fail to do so. Since both religious and non-religious practices can be insightful, and both can lack insight, I want to maximize wisdom by promoting the sharing of ideas. Since I assume that religions are too multifaceted to fit a single definition (whether or not one likes this situation), I find fuzzy set approaches useful to sort out the huge range of phenomena that can fit under the category 'religious'. Scholars who pursue this approach often notice that religions may articulate a sense of mystery, transcendence, and/or testing the limits of everyday perception. Such scholars also notice that religions often underline and cultivate what is considered most important – including matters of life and death, as well as the mystery of what forms of consciousness (or if not ordinary consciousness, then perhaps karma, spirit, or legacies of ancestors) may persist beyond death. Therefore, even though Björk's song does not fit all working definitions of religion – we could focus on other aspects of religion less relevant to her case – nevertheless, if we begin from a family resemblance approach and proceed to compare stances towards life in the face of death, we can easily place Björk in dialogue with unambiguously religious discourses. Emphatically, we should not assume that her song is anti-religious by definition.

Harris may not consider my response to Björk sufficiently scientific. True, I have studied religion for 30 years, so my judgement might count for something, but on the other hand I may have become polluted. So let us turn to another case:

> [Consider a] suicide bomber who blasts his way into paradise, expecting to be eternally entertained by seventy virgins . . . [or a Christian culture warrior] who eagerly expects to be raptured into Heaven . . . [to] a ringside seat whence he or she can watch the suffering of unbelievers during the Last Days. Not all religion is good; there is bad religion in the same way that there is bad art, bad cooking, and bad sex. In fact, religion is difficult to do well and we are seeing a lot of bad religion at the moment.[61]

What this quotation calls 'bad religion' is what Harris sees as the essence of religion. Presumably, he would agree that there are better and worse forms of cooking, but he puts religion in a separate category, which I have described in terms of an X trait overwhelming all others. In fact, I chose my opening example of computer viruses because new atheists often describe religion as a virus. They marvel that evolution allowed this virus to be naturally selected, perhaps because ancestors who easily perceived a lion's face on a rock, and by extension the faces of gods in clouds, were more likely to escape from real lions and pass on their genes to future generations (see William Calvin's Chapter 16). However, new atheists feel that this trait is now useless at best (like a human appendix) and often maladaptive, insofar as religion breeds ignorance and war (but see Maschner's Chapter 6 on the evolution of violence). Thus one critic notes that new atheists 'condemn not just belief in God but respect for belief in God. Religion is not only wrong: it's evil.'[62] Once again – since Harris wants to test claims against evidence – is this what religions are really like, if we approach them with reasonably broad and multilayered definitions?

New atheists insist that they do not lack humility, depth of imagination, appreciation for mysteries of the universe, or wonder in the face of beauty. Harris spends many pages defending mysticism, conceived as a rational and empirical enterprise and informed by Buddhist philosophy. Lest we expect this to lead towards respect for actual Buddhists, he explains that Buddhism 'is not a religion of faith, or a religion at all, in the Western sense' – despite 'millions of Buddhists who don't seem to know this, [who] can be found in temples . . . praying to Buddha as though he were a numinous incarnation of Santa Claus.'[63] Harris calls this a 'distortion of tradition,' which suggests some possibility that religions might evolve in directions that are useful to rational seekers after all. However, he states that 'non-dualistic empirical mysticism seems to have arisen only in the East.' Although 'the West has not been entirely bereft of wisdom,' Westerners are 'standing on the shoulders of dwarfs.'[64]

Whatever we think about this argument, Harris clearly has strong spiritual interests, and in general new atheists make persuasive claims about their sense of wonder and other such aspects of their worldviews – with an exception for their claim to humility. Somehow they know, without engaging with religious insiders at their strongest, that the imagination and nuance they recognize in themselves (articulated in non-religious languages) is qualitatively different from what religious insiders have long sought to articulate in other registers – some of the major cultural discourses that we have inherited from human history. Thus, although he grants that religious traditions are not 'entirely bereft of wisdom,' Harris insists on retooling this wisdom. What is rational is not religious, what is religious is not rational, and if a religious discourse claims to be evolving creatively (as successive stages of science have done) it must be moving away from religion. How does he know this? By definition.

New atheists outsmart themselves, at least if they desire to be effective in critiquing politically disturbing forms of religion. It is not entirely clear if Harris really cares about being effective; he may prefer a sense of elitist despair about the benighted masses. But he is right to worry about authoritarian religion. He is right to valorize Buddhist perspectives, and by extension other practices that are rational, constructive and rooted in religious traditions. Importantly, he is right to attack wishy-washy moderates who fail to confront the religious right because they are too busy making compromises that paper over basic conflicts. Not all moderates work to defeat behaviour X; many fail to confront authoritarian religion due to excessive concerns about tolerance. If Harris were not swinging so wildly, his criticism of this problem could be his strongest contribution.

Sadly, his arguments do more harm than good. He reinforces an idea near the root of the behaviour that worries him – the idea that *real* religion is an authoritarian Christian kind and that all liberals are its enemies. Harris and Christian fundamentalists agree on this. Moreover, conservatives feed off his attacks to strengthen their talking points about enemies who disrespect religion. In their mirror image of Harris's rhetoric, secularism is the polluting X factor. Insofar as we posit a zero-sum choice – religion versus reason – Harris supports the side that is likely to lose for the foreseeable future, at least in the US. Meanwhile, he foments divisions among religious and secular liberals, people who could deepen his Buddhist insights, and religious people of many stripes who presuppose rational methods and anti-authoritarian commitments.

Harris ends his book with a ringing call: 'Spiritual experience, ethical behaviour, and strong communities are essential for human happiness . . . it must be possible to bring reason, spirituality and ethics together.'[65] There is no reason why huge numbers of religious people like Martha, engaged in behaviour from A through everything except X, should not be Harris's allies in pursuing this goal – except that Harris excludes them by definition. Almost immediately after writing the above words, Harris asserts (despite a mountain of contrary evidence) that 'religious faith is the one species of human ignorance that will not admit of even the *possibility* of correction.'[66] It is hard to see how he can find a way, either out of this self-imposed blindness or the political impasse towards which it leads, unless he admits the possibility of adjusting his own definitions of what religion is and can be.

3 Aboriginal versus western creationism

Robert Layton

Social anthropologists are trained to work in cultures whose beliefs are very different to their own. Much of my own fieldwork has been carried out in Australian Aboriginal communities, far from the cities where most White Australians live. According to traditional Aboriginal belief, the world was shaped during an original, creative period often referred to in English as the 'Dreamtime', when figures with both human and animal qualities were active. As they travelled and encountered other such beings, the Python ancestors, the Kangaroo, Emu, the Dog and many other ancestral figures shaped the landscape. Where they camped, caves or waterholes were created. Where they met, the boundaries of clan territories were established. Their marriages, the gifts they gave each other and the fights that broke out among them provided a precedent for proper social relations today.

In considering whether scientists should confront religious beliefs, it may help to compare Aboriginal Australian beliefs with Creationism in the US, and ask why I am able to accept the Aboriginal beliefs as rational within their cultural context, but have more difficulty accepting the second.

In 1994, I returned to an Aboriginal community with whom I'd worked for several periods between 1979 and 1982. The community was living at Hodgson Downs, a pastoral station (cattle ranch) in the Northern Territory that had become available for a land claim by its traditional Aboriginal owners, the Alawa people. The Northern Territory Land Rights law of 1976 has a unique background. An earlier attempt by the Yolngu, another northern Aboriginal community, to claim legal ownership of their traditional country had failed in court, because the judge ruled Aboriginal people lacked any concept of ownership comparable to that of private property. In a generous spirit of multiculturalism (very different to the policies of the Australian government under John Howard from 1997 to 2007), the Federal government introduced a law defining Aboriginal land ownership as a collective responsibility of small groups descended from particular ancestors, who were entitled by Aboriginal tradition to hunt and gather over the land. To make a claim, an Aboriginal community had to provide evidence of its spiritual traditions, a map of the land claimed by each group, the groups' family trees, and evidence that people still used the land in a socially regulated way for hunting and gathering.

Thus it was that in 1994 that Bandiyan, a senior Alawa man I'd met 15 years earlier, was telling me the legend associated with a lagoon on the Hodgson River (see Figure 2) . It told how a group of dogs attacked and killed a goanna when the large lizard came to drink at the water's edge. Bandiyan pointed to the gum trees fringing the lagoon and explained, 'those trees are the Dogs waiting for the Goanna.' Perhaps I looked surprised, because he added, 'Not the young trees, the really old ones.' Bandiyan's explanation suddenly brought home to me how differently Aboriginal and European people envisage the World's age, and the scale of the transformation in European thought brought about by the

Figure 2 Aborigines, Hodgson Downs, Australia.

19th-century geological revolution when, 'Very suddenly, the bottom dropped out of history and its beginnings disappeared in an abyss of time'.[67] A few days later, I was visited by an old White Australian friend I'd not seen for ten years. A geologist by training, he was helping Aboriginal communities negotiate with mining companies. As we talked in the caravan lent me by the Hodgson Downs community I gradually realized my friend had become a creationist. When I finally balked at some remark, he challenged me, 'but how can you accept the Creationist beliefs of the Alawa, and not mine?'

Adaptation and belief

Now condemning creationists in the strongest of terms, Richard Dawkins previously made his name partly through coining the terms 'selfish gene' and 'selfish meme'. Dawkins argued that a gene exists only to perpetuate itself.[68] Over time, genes have cooperated in the evolution of the organisms that contain them and ensure their transmission from one generation to the next, but animals or plants are nothing more than 'gene machines'. In a similar way, Dawkins argued, cultural traits or *memes* are only concerned with their own reproduction. The fitness of memes is measured by their own success in spreading; they can be maladaptive for those who bear them. Cigarette smoking, drug taking and creationist beliefs are maladaptive memes that have nonetheless spread widely.

Against Dawkins, there are other theories for the evolution of culture (see Chapters 10 and 12 by Timothy Taylor and David Sloan Wilson), including the 'co-evolution' model,[69] which predicts that over tens of thousands of years humans have evolved to learn culture because it helped them adapt, live longer and have more children, who passed on these successful ideas. The co-evolution model assumes that maladaptive customs will be eliminated by selection against those who practice them. The anthropologist Marshall Sahlins[70] wrote that 'Culture is a gamble played with nature.' No culture is perfectly adapted to its environment, but if memes were generally maladaptive for their bearers, it seems plausible to predict that natural selection would tend to give humans a resistance to culture.

Is it possible, then, that creationist beliefs may be adaptive? This question raises two points. First, genes and memes are only adaptive in specific environments. Second, humans are highly social animals; they must adapt not just to their physical environment but also to other people and their social resources. There is no point in evolving a capacity for language, or friendship, if there are no other people!

Aboriginal ways of talking about the landscape

Aboriginal people could only survive by hunting and gathering through a detailed knowledge of their natural resources. Exchanging information about where resources are and planning cooperative foraging are vital abilities.[71] Biologists who have worked with Australia's indigenous communities recognize their remarkably fine-grained knowledge of their environment and the species within it.[72]

Hodgson Downs, in the Northern Territory of Australia, is dominated by open savannah woodland vegetation, while grassland covers the black soil river plains that flood every Wet Season. As the water retreats, the rivers become chains of lagoons and waterholes. Lagoons and their banks are the richest in useful species, and the suitability for foraging decreases moving up to the woodlands and higher up into the cliff country. The boundaries between clan territories frequently follow cliffs and watersheds. Water is intrinsically important for human survival and permanent reservoirs support the majority of subsistence resources.

Alawa orient themselves within their environment according to two principles, the position of the Sun and the direction of river flow:

Ngunakadi	Sunrise side	(East)
Lurunggadi	Sunset side	(West)

Since the prevailing direction of river flow is from south to north, Alawa directional terms upstream and downstream tend to correspond, fortuitously, to south and north:

Werdi	Upstream
Lenjeri	Downstream

A detailed terminology for describing the landscape exists in the Alawa language, for example:

Urai or Wuran	Blacksoil
Mangguru	Open plain
Lirrimunja	Ironstone/gravel ridge country
Namurlmiyn	Round Hill
Ngayiwurr	Cliff country

Travels of the creative ancestors

During my work on the Hodgson Downs land claim, I realized that both the routes of ancestral beings and the clan territories corresponded to the ecology of the landscape. Unlike Western property rights, the Alawa were often vague about exactly where one clan territory ended and another began, except at rivers, where estate boundaries are precisely defined. On a map, the routes of the ancestral beings generally followed rivers, creeks or valleys during their travel, because, in fact, they moulded these features. A sacred tree, rock or waterhole will be known to mark the 'last place' in a given estate, as often the ancestors released springs or dug wells in their search for water. When crossing dry rocky country, the ancestors did not normally stop. Major rivers are thus divided into blocs representing clan territories. Sometimes the being who formed one territory would turn back if he encountered another at work nearby. Each territory typically extends up tributary creeks and peters out at a watershed.

Rights to territory

The routes travelled by ancestral beings, and the sites they created across the landscape, direct how spiritual responsibilities are allocated to people. Alawa people are not only normally members of their father's clan, but also must ensure the correct performance of the ceremonies to commemorate the ancestors in their mother's clan. Most ancestors travelled extensively, and each clan has to re-enact the episodes within its territory. No one else can visit the clan's most sacred sites. Animating spirits of unborn children were left at certain points in the landscape by the ancestral heroes, usually pools of water. The child is said to have been 'soaked in the water' of the place where its spirit lay prior to conception. A child resides in the father's territory.

These rules are not, however, followed unthinkingly. Alawa recognize that premature deaths, or the failure to produce sons, may threaten the clan's survival. Some territories lost their Aboriginal owners during European colonization of the late 19th-and early 20th-centuries, as massacres forced surviving families to flee, while others sought food and work on cattle ranches. Sometimes related clans would give one or two young men to be trained in the traditions of a depleted group. Sometimes a child was conceived far from the father's country, giving it potential membership of the clan owning that site.

Aboriginal causal theories

In addition to celebrating the journeys of the ancestors, the clan must look after its territory. At the start of the Dry Season, dead grass and fallen branches are burned to prevent bush fires, to make it easier to walk, and to allow fresh grass to spring up as food for kangaroos. Rites are performed at the ancestors' sacred sites: the rock which is the transformed body of the Lizard must be struck to make plenty of lizards; the round stones that are the Python's eggs must be rescued from where floods carried them and put back in the hollow that is the Python's nest.

According to Aboriginal theory, matter and energy are interchangeable. The sacred sites are where the ancestors' creative power, as life-giving beings, was transformed into matter. Other rituals turn matter back into creative energy. It all serves as an indigenous geomorphology, explaining the origin of an environment on whose everyday properties indigenous and Western people basically agree.

In northern and central Australia, territorial rights help resolve two ecological conflicts. Sacred sites tend to be near water[73] because water lies in patches that are easy to defend, and because defence of sacred sites also dramatizes social relations that assist in times of drought.[74] Animal and plant foods, on the other hand, are dispersed over relatively unpredictable locations. People are entitled to forage well beyond their own territory (with permission and not trespassing on sacred sites), because it is more adaptive to allow non-exclusive, reciprocal rights to hunt and gather, as this allows everyone to benefit from temporary surpluses and escape local famine. The complex network of criss-crossing routes created by ancestral heroes reaffirms the interdependence of local groups. The historical and causal bases of these beliefs are beyond test, given the limits on Indigenous science.

Aboriginal versus Western Creationism

Writing before its resurgence under George W. Bush's government, Eve and Harrold[75] argued that Creationism in the US had persisted among a particular social class in relatively isolated communities. Social cleavages had coincided to separate creationists from mainstream US society. Indigenous Australians also live marginally in relation to the dominant colonial society, in ethnically distinct, often remote communities. Only through issues such as land rights do indigenous beliefs confront the dominant community. The most widely accepted argument for indigenous land rights is that they 'help Aboriginals generally keep their culture and help their survival'.[76] Many Australians, whether for or against land rights, contend that hunting, foraging and ceremony are not productive uses of the land. Aboriginal land rights are often seen as unfair to White Australians, who were denied the opportunity to claim land on the same basis.

Indigenous Australian beliefs provide an intellectually satisfying ontology, within the limits of empirical investigation practically available to believers, and a rational ground for action in the world. In this sense, they can be compared to the beliefs of creationists in the US, who are often intelligent, well-educated people, whose 'rules for knowing', particularly concerning issues of ultimate meaning, are different from those of evolutionists.[77] Similarly, just as Creationism in the US is used to justify moral stances (on human relations, abortion and stem cell research), the ethical aspect of Aboriginal 'Creationism' is regarded as one of its most attractive features (although their sense of rootedness in an ancient landscape, conveyed in Aboriginal art, also has a romantic appeal).

However, although both groups similarly seek tolerant recognition in a dominant community, the 'Western' creationists further demand we accede to a truth that deserves equal exposure to evolutionary theory in the country's schools and universities.[78] Creationism in the US was promoted before a wider audience as part of Karl Rove's election strategy for George W. Bush. Rove's strategy has been to destroy the middle-ground consensus in US politics, in the expectation that more voters will move to the right than to the left. Creationism becomes part of mainstream political debate. Karl Rove is not irrational.

Dawkins' dismissal of Creationism as a maladaptive, empirically false 'meme' overlooks its social functions. My astonishment at my geologist friend advocating Creationism at Hodgson Downs arose because I am persuaded that the empirical evidence for natural selection far outweighs the claims of the biblical *Book of Genesis.* Yet I respected Aboriginal beliefs because I appreciated how they legitimize their rights and organize survival and social life in a difficult environment. Dawkins' naïve conviction that people in the US will change their beliefs – if insulted volubly enough – fails to recognize how those beliefs – however misguided and regrettable – support their morality and sense of alienation from elite politics.

4 Science versus anthropology, not religion

Simon Coleman

When asked to write for this book, my original question was whether scientists should *contest* religious beliefs, rather than *challenge* them as Part I is titled now. I think the original wording is perhaps more useful for me, as my initial response was to reflect on two rather different incidents of contestation from my past. The first occurred some 20 years ago, when I was doing fieldwork in a Protestant, charismatic ministry in Sweden. The ministry ran a flourishing university student group, and one night I went along to a meeting and learned that its leader was going to address his audience on the topic of academic disciplines. His question was: 'Which ones should born-again, Bible-believing Christians study and which should they avoid?' 'Here we go,' I thought, 'biologists and physicists are going to get it in the neck.' But actually the speaker explained it was fine to be a natural scientist, or indeed a lawyer, or an economist. Two disciplines, however, were beyond the pale. One was theology: after all, it might talk a lot about God but it tended to analyse Him out of existence. The other, I'm afraid to say, was anthropology: and what the speaker really didn't like about that discipline was that it was *comparative*: why should a proper Christian spend time reflecting on religious systems that were so plainly wrong, and which talked of gods rather than the one God?

That was the first incident. The second occured 10 years later, at a meeting of the American Anthropological Association in San Francisco. Leslie Carlin and I had put together a panel called the 'Cultures of Creationism,' aimed at discussing the preconditions for successful creationist movements: why were they popular in some parts of the English-speaking world, but largely ignored in others? All was going in line with our expectations – although we had a surprisingly large audience for the first session on a Sunday morning – until we threw open the floor to discussion and questions. What we found was that our musings on cultural context turned pretty swiftly to debates about cultural politics and policies. The audience wanted to know how anthropologists could deal with creationist ideas held by students and promulgated by school boards – they were asking whether anthropologists should be more aggressive in attempting to take over forums on public debate. And so on.[79] This was a passionate as well as an intellectual interest, fuelled by heated debates and challenges in classrooms and newspapers.

Both of these incidents involved a *contest* within a group that was ostensibly on the same side of an issue. What is actually opposed is revealing. My charismatic lecturer objected not to natural science, but to social science; not to 'facts' but to comparing ideas that he would preferred to be separated by a hierarchy. Meanwhile, the anthropologists in San Francisco welcomed a rare opportunity to forget their usual cross-cultural comparisons in favour of working out strategies to defend their own discipline.

These events point to a useful ambiguity over whether scientists should contest or defend religious beliefs: do we mean *natural* scientists or *social* scientists, or should it make no difference? We can talk about the meanings of 'belief' till we're blue in the face (as Lewis Wolpert essentially says in Chapter 8), but what about the assumptions behind the word 'contest'? What might be the rules, the meanings, behind different kinds – cultures – of contestation? Perhaps instead of talking of science versus anthropology, social scientists should be more confident in what they do. That confidence should lead us – perhaps paradoxically – to the avoidance of one kind of contestation and the promotion of another.

I recently read an intriguing newspaper article: 'Top scientist gives up on creationists'. In his talk, 'Why Creationism is Wrong and Evolution is Right' at the 2006 Hay-on-Wye book festival, evolutionary biologist Steve Jones announced that debating with creationists was a waste of time. A journalist commented that 'One is left wishing that the 100 m American creationists – or the one in three people in the UK who allegedly believe that the universe was designed – could be made to listen to him talk. Surely even they would find it difficult to resist him.'[80] Well, I have little doubt that the vast majority of those 100 million would have had no problem resisting Steve Jones, charismatic and forceful speaker though he is, and it is our job as socio-cultural anthropologists to know why.

Cultures of contestation

If you look at past debates over evolution you see that contestation – or the anguished avoidance of it – comes up again and again. Darwin is said to have avoided publishing for fear of provoking his wife and/ or the Church. 'Darwin's bulldog', Thomas Henry Huxley, is said to have humiliated an intellectually challenged Bishop Wilberforce in Oxford in 1860. The Scopes trial, mentioned by Gordy Slack, was supposedly about an enlightened lawyer humiliating a reactionary evangelical. Theologians such as Alister McGrath[81] refer to the 'warfare' of science and religion, and 19th-century examples have plenty of contemporary counterparts in accounts of School Boards in Georgia or even Gateshead. The model has also gained new strength over the past 40 years or so as evangelicals in the US and beyond have attempted to reclaim public intellectual and political space from so-called secular humanism.

This warfare model is also evident when a Steve Jones or a Richard Dawkins debates evolutionary theory with creationists, and also in how writers such as Dawkins juxtapose religion and science. So for Dawkins, scientific beliefs get 'results', whereas religious faiths do not; religion is a kind of mind virus; and people can move towards science as they are persuaded of its inherent superiority.[82] In *The Devil's Chaplain*, Dawkins argues that religion and science cannot converge, because religions still make claims about the world – such as miracles – which turn out to be scientific claims: 'Theologians, if they want to remain honest, should make a choice. You can claim your own magisterium, separate from science's but still deserving of respect . . . Or you can keep your Lourdes and your miracles, and enjoy their huge recruiting potential among the uneducated. But then you must kiss goodbye to separate magisteria and your high-minded aspiration to converge on science.'[83] The implication is that the scientist must decide what science is, while the believer decides what religion is. But to establish two different *magisteria* (Latin for 'master's offices') implies some intellectual convergence, or mutually agreed criteria for the division of ideas.

While Dawkins has his own distinctive voice, it is also worth stepping back a bit to look at the intellectual context of his writing. The theologian John Milbank argues that Dawkins' position is part of the wider 'mythos' of secular reason – whether Marxist, liberal, post-modern and so on – that has come to dominate modern thought. But there are parallels with another vision of rationality, that of Ernest Gellner, who in 1992 preached in King's College Chapel, Cambridge on 'The Uniqueness of Truth'.[84] The theme had occupied him all his life – how Truth can be approached given the treacheries of language and the pluralities of human culture – and I think it is relevant today. Gellner described three categories of modern ideological authority: The [religious] fundamentalist, the Enlightenment puritan and the relativist. The first two share a sense of the uniqueness of Truth; whereas the Enlightenment puritan and the relativist share a penchant for tolerance. The relativist and the fundamentalist inhabit worlds much more comfortable than the arid, empty world of the Enlightenment puritan. Gellner reckoned that many anthropologists belonged to the relativist camp. He saw himself, however, as a card-carrying, Enlightenment Puritan, a follower of what he called 'rationalist fundamentalism' – the conviction that all claims of 'truth' must be judged by generic, disinterested procedures for reliably investigating the world. He also – like Dawkins – presented his own idea of pollution, in his case post-modernists as peddlers of a virulent form of 'conceptual intoxicant', which echoes Dawkins' description of 'fatuous' relativists as opposed to the 'sensible' ones.[85]

Both Gellner and Dawkins, then, construct a similar kind of contest, in a similar way. A proper contest needs everybody to accept the same rules of engagement, since all appear to be competing for the prize of 'truth'. These rules include an assumption that people mean what they say rather directly, and also that a uniform entity called *science* can debate with a uniform entity called *religion*, with both reasonably represented by their elite spokesmen and women.

I suspect both Dawkins and Gellner would at least respect the evangelist Robert Horton Gundry's[86] robust assertion that some ways of thinking are better than others (even if disagreeing with his actual ideas). There is an awful lot to be said for such contestation, which implies a respect for the opponent, and allows for direct comparisons of modes of thought. For instance, by permitting comparison between Western and non-Western cultures, it encourages us to look at Western evangelicals and their theories of creation much as we would Australian aboriginal theories (see Robert Layton's Chapter 3) or indeed Cosmology (David Wilkinson's Chapter 18). But are the assumptions about the rules of engagement and contestation comprehensive enough? Let's assume for today's purposes that we have a pretty good idea of the intentions of Dawkins or Gundry or Gellner as they support what they see as a rational view of the Universe. What can we say about the role of say evolutionary theory, as well as the culture of contestation, within religious systems such as Protestant evangelicalism?

We can start with one of the necessary points of contact between religion and science. The depiction of religion as *mental activity* has a significant history. In the early 18th-century, Deist philosophy, with its view that God does not interfere with human life or the laws of the Universe, freed the great truths of religion from any particular historical events of revelation. This perspective not only paved the way for modern religions, it also encouraged the perceived divergence between magic, religion and science – which had not been distinct concepts before the Enlightenment – as separate ideologies. By the late 19th-century, the anthropologist Edward Tylor simply described religion as 'the belief in Spiritual Beings'. For anthropologists, 'religion' had become encapsulated as a widely understood cultural category, with local instances that could be compared with each other.

Total separation between anthropology and religion was never possible, however – anthropologists came from religious backgrounds (Tylor from Protestant nonconformist stock), and Christian fundamentalism itself began to formalize the faith as a set of universal principles. Yet, the term 'belief' as a specific way of viewing the world has no counterpart in the language of many societies and so cannot be universally defined across all cultures. Even a faith such as Western Christian fundamentalism is not only a standard system of thought, but is also locally embodied in buildings, practices and principles.

Nor should anthropologists always take religious ideologies literally. In my work on Protestantism, for instance, I see how language can serve multiple purposes as believers negotiate their way through different cultures. A pastor might use civil language in secular contexts, but reinterpret those words in a church service. Phrases can have one significance for secular interlocutors and another for believers. I've termed this linguistic strategy 'double-talk', where the natural and supernatural worlds are parallel, but not always in synch with each other. The point is that the language ideology in a debate on evolution may not be the same for everyone. Even a claim that Genesis must be taken literally requires us to understand what is meant by 'literally'. Indeed, part of the very problem for an anthropologist studying evangelicalism is not to take for granted words that are all too familiar.

Of course, the meaning of language is not entirely relative, and we cannot simply dismiss others' words as 'merely' expressive or symbolic and insert our own meanings. After interviews with believing natural scientists, the Christian anthropologist Karla Poewe[87] argued that their doing science and knowing God through the Holy Spirit were connected by similar patterns of thought. But my point is that creationist debate with secularists needs to be viewed in relation to conservative Protestantism as a whole. An example Leslie Carlin and I gave in our introduction to the book *The Cultures of Creationism* was provided by an interview with Bob Willis, head of the Creation Science Association for Mid-America, for the *New Scientist* (2000:41–3). Asked how he came to be converted to creationism, Willis replies that it was partly through reading Darwin, but also in the following way:

> I was not a Christian – I didn't know Christianity from the sole of my foot. But I became a creationist – an anti-evolutionist Christian – by a series of,

> some would say, unusual events. One was a traumatic personal event that caused me to rethink the meaning of life and to seek other solutions from the lifestyle I was living.

Willis's commitment to Creationism is not about simple intellectual persuasion changing his ideas; his description is phrased in the classic evangelical language of conversion, whereby ignorance is followed by trauma and a changed perspective on the world. Creationism here is more than a set of ideas – it is embodied in practices that go beyond debates about Genesis, which are presented as having been constitutive of the speaker as a believing person; indeed Creationism takes on a further iconic character when subsequently expressed in the language of witness.

These examples indicate the loaded nature of cultural and religious translation: whether by anthropologists defining religion, biologists debating the role of religion in evolutionary theory or creationists representing their arguments in seemingly secular contexts. Engagement in the contest involves tensions over the rules of contestation from different cultural perspectives. 'Muted groups', as Shirley Ardener calls them, adopt the language of the powerful in order to be heard but, in doing so, place themselves within arenas that undermine their case from the very beginning. Imagine Richard Dawkins explaining evolutionary theory in the idiom of Jerry Falwell or Pat Robertson and you get a sense of what I mean. Although creationists often bring this situation upon themselves, the interesting question is not whether they are 'right' or 'wrong': far more intriguing is what *they* feel they are doing, how they perceive the contest and the public appealed to. Indeed, creation science is, like most conversionist rhetoric, unlikely to convince anyone in itself, because such commitment emerges through social and kin relationships combined with certain life experiences. What is important for many believers is that the message is seen to be projected into public space, occupying that space – however briefly – with Christian personalities and ideas. Indeed, the opprobrium attracted from the likes of Richard Dawkins can assist in such self-projection – an indication of the provocative power of the Christian message.

So what of the question of whether scientists should contest religion? My argument is that, from the point of view of the social scientist, the battle over 'truth' is unresolvable because each side contests with a different set of rules. Our job as ethnographers is to probe, to question, and to combine sympathy and distance. The situation is otherwise for a Richard Dawkins or a Steve Jones whose intellectual agenda is entirely different; but they would be mistaken if they assumed they would influence many of their opponents through their arguments. Theirs is an idiom of persuasion with its own rhetorical force, but it is not a force that makes sense within evangelical circles. Dawkins exclaims that 'It is time for people of intellect, as opposed to people of faith, to stand up and say "Enough!"'[88] But is it enough, even in Dawkins' own terms, to simply preach to the converted using familiar idioms?

We need to develop an anthropology not only of 'Creationism' but also of 'Dawkinism' as a cultural phenomenon that takes certain rhetorical forms, including the need to contest another discourse seen as trespassing on scientific practice and thus deserving of scorn. Our job is to identify the politics of what one might call the political economy of knowledge.

For the teacher of anthropology confronted by the creationist, mere argument will not suffice. The confrontation in the classroom is not a place for easy consensus. But there is a difference between doing ethnography and spreading the message of anthropology. Discovering and exploring the world of another is not the same as explaining – indeed promulgating – the disciplinary world in which many of use choose to live. There is a public role for the social anthropologist, but it does not consist in attacking any one religion or cultural system. It consists instead of arguing for the need to understand as far as possible the world of the other before it's possible to frame the idea of a conversation or even a contest that will have any lasting influence.

5 Atheism and liberty

Michael Shermer

Over the past several years the traditionally staid and academic field of science-and-religion studies has erupted in a paroxysm of public debate and disputation, landing theists and atheists on magazine covers and bestseller lists. Much has been made in the popular press about the angry attacks on religion by atheists and scientists, most notably by Richard Dawkins (*The God Delusion*), Daniel Dennett (*Breaking the Spell*), Sam Harris (*The End of Faith* and *Letter to a Christian Nation*) and Christopher Hitchens (*God is Not Great*). I know all of these gentlemen quite well, consider them good friends, and agree with their arguments and conclusions on the God question. Indeed, I've made most of these arguments in my belief trilogy (*Why People Believe Weird Things*, *How We Believe* and *The Science of Good and Evil*), yet I am often cast as a moderate for my more conciliatory approach towards religion. What is the right tactic to take? The answer depends on what one wants to accomplish.

Since the turn of the millennium a new militancy has arisen among religious sceptics in response to three threats to science and freedom: (1) evolution education and stem cell research, (2) breaks in the barrier separating church and state leading to political preferences for some faiths over others and (3) fundamentalist terrorism here and abroad. In addition, they loudly and proudly proclaim that it is okay to be an atheist, and they free the burden of having to respect others' beliefs when they don't respect ours. Dawkins' programme of 'consciousness raising' is laudable and liberating. He wants to 'raise consciousness to the fact that to be an atheist is a realistic aspiration, and a brave and splendid one. You can be an atheist who is happy, balanced, moral, and intellectually fulfilled.' He wants atheists to quit apologizing for their religious scepticism. 'On the contrary, it is something to be proud of, standing tall to face the far horizon, for atheism nearly always indicates a healthy independence of mind and, indeed, a healthy mind.' Amen, brother.

Without question, whenever religious beliefs conflict with scientific facts or violate principles of political liberty, we must respond with appropriate aplomb. I understand and often share atheists' anger in the teeth of so much religious intolerance in today's society, especially the breathtakingly asinine notion that atheists are inherently incapable of being moral and dignified people and citizens. As a 1999 Gallup poll found, a gay Black woman could be elected president before an atheist could, an appalling fact for a modern liberal democracy. In point of fact, studies show that atheists are just as (if not more) moral than theists, even studies conducted by the Christian pollster George Barna. In his 1996 *Index of Leading Spiritual Indicators*, Barna noted: 'Born again Christians continue to have a higher likelihood of getting divorced [27 per cent] than do non-Christians [24 per cent].' In a 2001 survey, Barna found '33 per cent of all born again individuals who have been married have gone through a divorce, which is statistically identical to the 34 per cent incidence among non-born again adults.' A tie.

More broadly, in a 2005 study published in the *Journal of Religion and Society* – 'Cross-National Correlations of Quantifiable Societal Health with Popular Religiosity and Secularism in the Prosperous Democracies' – independent scholar Gregory S. Paul found an inverse correlation between religiosity (measured by belief in God, biblical literalism, and frequency of prayer and service attendance) and societal health (measured by rates of homicide, suicide, childhood mortality, life expectancy, sexually transmitted diseases, abortion and teen pregnancy) in 18 developed democracies. 'In general, higher rates of belief in and worship of a creator correlate with higher rates of homicide, juvenile and early adult mortality, STD infection rates, teen pregnancy, and abortion in the prosperous democracies,' Paul found. 'The United States is almost always the most dysfunctional of the developed democracies, sometimes spectacularly so.' Indeed, the US scores the highest in religiosity and the highest (by far) in homicides, STDs, abortions and teen pregnancies. Despite being the most religious nation of the sample (not to mention the most economically prosperous), the US is at or near the bottom of every societal health measure.

The prejudices against us persist anyway. In America, atheists are associated with tree-hugging, whale-saving, hybrid-driving, bottled water-drinking, American Civil Liberties Union-supporting, pinko commie fags hell-bent on conning our youth into believing all that baloney about equal rights and evolution. When we hear such sentiments, we should not hesitate to respond, ala Howard Beale in the 1976 film *Network*, by sticking our collective heads out of our windows and shouting 'I'm mad as hell and I'm not going to take this any more.'

Nevertheless, we must be cautious not to let this atheist reward-centre stroking turn into the same form of intolerance and superiority to which we are often subjected. I wince when I hear religious people referred to as 'faith-heads' and 'clowns,' as being less intelligent or poorly reasoned, or worse, deluded. I cringe when I hear their religious beliefs compared to cancer, or to smoking cigarettes. And I grimace when religious moderates are called enablers of terrorism, their doctrines identified as Bronze Age relics and the equation of prayer to talking to a hairdryer.

I shudder because I have many religious friends and colleagues who do not in the least fit these descriptions – they are thoughtful, intelligent, educated people who abhor terrorism, who engage in prayer mainly for contemplative (not petitionary) purposes and whose religions may have Bronze Age origins but are thoroughly modern in structure. I empathize at the pain such pejorative appellations cause them.

We need to raise our consciousness a little higher. Dawkins asks us, pace John Lennon, to 'imagine no religion': 'no suicide bombers, no 9/11, no 7/7, no Crusades, no witch-hunts, no Gunpowder Plot, no Indian partition, no Israeli/Palestinian wars, no Serb/Croat/Muslim massacres, no persecution of Jews as "Christ-killers", no Northern Ireland "troubles", no "honour killings", no shiny-suited bouffant-haired televangelists fleecing gullible people of their money . . .'

Indeed, all these, and more, we plainly could do without. But in my opinion many of these events – and others often attributed solely to religion by atheists – were less religiously motivated than politically driven, or at the very least involved religion in the service of political hegemony. History, like life, is usually multivariate in its causes and consequences. And, I wonder, without religion, who would take care of the poor, the needy, the starving, the diseased and the destitute? My atheist friends respond: 'the government'. The government? you mean like they did for the victims of Katrina? As they have for inner-city slums and single-parent families?

According to Syracuse University professor Arthur C. Brooks in his 2006 book *Who Really Cares*, when it comes to charitable giving and volunteering numerous quantitative measures debunk the myth of 'bleeding heart liberals' and 'heartless conservatives'. Religious conservatives donate 30 per cent more money than liberals (even when controlled for income), give more blood and log more volunteer hours. In general, religious people are four times more generous than secularists to all charities, 10 per cent more munificent to non-religious charities and 57 per cent more likely than a secularist to help a homeless person. Those raised in intact and religious families are more charitable than those who are not. In terms of societal health, charitable givers are 43 per cent more likely to say they are 'very happy' than nongivers and 25 per cent more likely than nongivers to say their health is 'excellent' or 'very good'. Before we imagine a world without religion (or possessions?), we need to consider what social institutions will be substituted for all the good that religion does.

Instead of focusing our energy on eradicating religion, consider the following observations and principle.

1. *The Power of Positive Assertions.* Atheists champion science, reason and rationality, which are best promoted through positive assertions. Here I take advice from Charles Darwin who, in 1880, clarified his reasoning on the question of science and religion to Edward Aveling, the noted British socialist. Aveling had solicited Darwin's endorsement of a group of radical atheists by asking his

permission to dedicate a book Aveling edited entitled *The Student's Darwin*, a collection of articles discussing the implications of evolutionary theory for religious thought. The book had a militant anti-religious flavour that Darwin disdained and he declined the offer, elaborating his reason with his usual flare for quotable maxims:

> It appears to me (whether rightly or wrongly) that direct arguments against christianity & theism produce hardly any effect on the public; & freedom of thought is best promoted by the gradual illumination of men's minds which follow[s] from the advance of science. It has, therefore, been always my object to avoid writing on religion, & I have confined myself to science.

2. *Anti-Something Movements are Doomed to Failure.* We cannot simply define ourselves by what do not believe, a principle I learned from the great Austrian economist and classical liberal Ludwig von Mises, who in 1956 warned his anti-Communist colleagues:

   > An anti-something movement displays a purely negative attitude. It has no chance whatever to succeed. Its passionate diatribes virtually advertise the program they attack. People must fight for something that they want to achieve, not simply reject an evil, however bad it may be.

3. *Rational Consciousness Raising.* If it is our goal to raise the consciousness of as many people as possible to the wonders of science, the power of reason, and the virtues of rationality, we must apply science, reason, and rationality to our actions, not just our ideas. It is irrational to take an angry, hostile, demeaning, belittling or condescending attitude towards religion. By so doing we virtually guarantee that religious people will, in response, adopt an angry, hostile, demeaning, belittling or condescending attitude towards science, reason and rationality. In other words, our negative actions will have the exact opposite effect that we wish them to have, which is what makes them irrational. Here I am not hypocritically pointing fingers, for I have been as guilty as anyone of biting and sardonic

rejoinders to religious claims and people; instead I wish to call attention to what I see as a misdirection that our movement has taken. As Carl Sagan cautioned us in *Demon-Haunted World*: 'You can get into a habit of thought in which you enjoy making fun of all those other people who don't see things as clearly as you do. We have to guard carefully against it.'

We must direct our outrage at specific targets and heed the words of the greatest consciousness raiser of the 20th-century, Martin Luther King, Jr, in his now canonized 'I Have a Dream' speech:

> In the process of gaining our rightful place, we must not be guilty of wrongful deeds. Let us not seek to satisfy our thirst for freedom by drinking from the cup of bitterness and hatred. We must forever conduct our struggle on the high plane of dignity and discipline.

By the virtue of the golden rule, if we do not want theists to prejudge atheists in a negative light, then atheists must not do unto theists the same.

To this end I would like to propose that we raise our consciousness towards a higher goal that encompasses both science and religion, that allows for the free expression of both belief and disbelief, and in which science, reason, and rationality are subsumed within a broader principle, the *Principle of Freedom: all people are free to think, believe and act as they choose, as long as they do not infringe on the equal freedom of others.*

This was the Enlightenment programme as put into practice by Messrs Paine, Jefferson and Mill, and carried on ever since by freedom fighters everywhere. With a higher goal of spreading liberty and freedom to more people in more places, science, reason and rationality become the means towards an end, not ends in themselves.

With the Principle of Freedom in hand, we can see why we should be tolerant of religion: not because we want to 'make nice' (which is patronizing); not because it is the polite thing to do in a polite society (true enough, but not good enough); and not because science fosters open discussion and dissent (it does, but we can reach higher still). We should conduct our struggle on the high plane of dignity and discipline because it is the rational thing to do: if we want the freedom to disbelieve, then we must grant others the freedom to believe. If it is our higher goal to attenuate intolerance, to expand the sphere of freedom to encompass all peoples, and to accentuate the free expression of both belief and disbelief, then the freedom of atheists not to worship God is inextricably bound to the freedom of theists to worship God. As Dr King noted:

> The marvellous new militancy which has engulfed the Negro community must not lead us to a distrust of all white people, for many of our white brothers, as evidenced by their presence here today, have come to realize that their destiny is tied up with our destiny. And they have come to realize that their freedom is inextricably bound to our freedom.

Read atheists for Negro and theists for White people. Then let freedom ring.

Part II Is religion inevitable? Prehistory and evolution

6 The evolution of warfare

Herbert D. G. Maschner and Katherine L. Reedy-Maschner

We often wonder, given the state of the modern world, if there is not some deep, unnerving, even insidious relationship between religion and war. A primary indictment of religion is the fact that in the last 3,000 years, hundreds of millions of people have been killed in the name of the Judeo-Christian-Islamic God, conflicts continuing today in the Middle East, north Africa, India, Malaysia, northern Ireland and in isolated events across the US. The worldly success of these major religions has included a powerful military component; from David's capture and defence of Jerusalem in the early 1st millennium BC, to the Islamic expansion across the Mediterranean in the 8th century AD, the Crusades of the early 2nd millennium AD against Islam, the often violent missionization of indigenous peoples during colonization, the attempts by Fascist Christians to eradicate Judaism in the late 2nd millennium, to the rise of modern Fundamentalism. Yes, the relationship between war and belief has a long and ugly common history, but is religion itself actually the *cause* of war or simply another excuse for humans to create artificial differences – 'us' versus 'them' – to justify the violence they use to solve other issues of humanness?

No one knows when the first religion came into being, or even when the mind evolved to the complexity necessary to create such abstract symbolism. But sometime between about 100,000 and 45,000 years ago, as Steven Mithen discusses, there was a universal reorganization of the early human brain such that symbols of belief, seen mostly in art drawn on cave walls or worn as jewellery, and a belief in the afterlife as seen in burials, came into being and quickly changed the face of human society forever. Throughout this same period, we have evidence of human violence – skulls crushed from club blows and spear points embedded in human bones – showing all was not peaceful during the earliest belief in the supernatural.

It would be convenient to end the argument at this point by simply recognizing that religion and interpersonal violence have always existed side by side. But in this case, we must go back further. Long before the creation of religion, or even the cognitive ability to be religious, human violence was present. The ability of humans and their early ancestors to organize into groups of males with a common goal and aggressively seek out other humans and kill them has deep evolutionary roots that are not directly linked to religious ideals.

Long before religion, language, or even the development of formal weaponry, we suspect small groups of Australopithecines, 3.5-million-year-old ancestors to modern humans, conducted boarder patrols, maintained territories and killed rivals over mates. We know this because sometime between 10 and 6 million years ago, humans and chimpanzees split on the evolutionary tree. Humans and chimpanzees share many similar behaviours, including those that allow us to organize into lethal groups, a trait that logically must be ancestral to both species. These behaviours evidently evolved after the human–chimpanzee common ancestor split from the line leading to modern gorillas, because gorillas do not share those same characteristics.

As Harvard anthropologist Richard Wrangham wrote with Dale Peterson in *Demonic Males*[89]

> the single most gripping set of facts about chimpanzee behavior is . . . the nature of their society. The social world of chimpanzees is a set of individuals who share a common communal range; males live forever in the groups where they were born, while females move to neighboring groups at adolescence; and the range is defended, and sometimes extended with aggressive and potentially lethal violence, by groups of males related in a genetically patrilineal kin group . . . Very few animals live in male bonded, patrilineal communities . . . and only two are known to do so with a system of intense, male-initiated territorial aggression, including lethal raiding into neighboring communities in search of vulnerable enemies to attack and kill.

Out of millions of animal species, Wrangham and Peterson point out, this suite of behaviours is unique to chimpanzees and humans. Part of a deep cognitive psychology, they are a product of a common evolutionary history. If chimpanzees organize into violent groups with no obvious 'religion' belief system, should we end this discussion right here? There would seem to be no evolutionary relationship between warfare and religion.

Not so fast.

One of the primary evolutionary changes in the history of all mammals was the ability to compete with others, especially for mates. So many higher species do this that few animal scientists doubt that male–male competition is critical to evolution in general. But what many overlook, as David Sloan Wilson discusses in Chapter 12, is the evolution of cooperation, especially among males. Without the ability to cooperate, warfare could not exist. We believe that the evolution of cooperation is the single most important event in the evolution of warfare.

Some see prehistoric hunting as the precursor to warfare, since chimpanzees and humans both cooperate in hunting activities. But as primatologist Frans de Waal writes,[90] 'feeding has very little to do with aggression . . . The neural circuitry of the two patterns is different: the first expresses fear and aggression, the second is motivated by hunger'. Only some groups of chimpanzees hunt, whereas all common chimpanzees participate in group-level violence against other groups of chimpanzees. This suggests that organized violence evolved before organized hunting, and that cooperation ability coevolved with group violence.

In the evolutionary world of our early hominine ancestors, 3 million or more years ago, males were larger in order to compete for mates, defend those mates and defend their offspring. Scavenging and hunting were probably very important and, much like their chimpanzee ancestors, maintaining territorial boundaries and patrolling those boundaries was critical to a group's success.

What evidence is there for the earliest organized violence? Very few early fossils demonstrate interpersonal conflict, but realistically, we would not expect to see much. Imagine extraterrestrial archaeologists arriving in the US and a PhD student is planning to excavate a random sample of 20th-century burials. There is a trivial chance that this archaeologist would find any evidence that Americans participated in warfare during the 20th-century, even with well-preserved remains.[91]

Now go back 3 million years and the fossil record is so barely preserved, such a tiny remainder of events that occurred, that we cannot count on witnessing interpersonal violence. But if it was indeed present so long ago, then through archaeological time, with more fossils and better preservation, we should find more evidence for violence and warfare. This is indeed the case.

For several million years, as our ancestors expanded across the east African savannas, small groups of cooperating males were led by an alpha male of sorts, much like their chimpanzee relatives. After 500,000 years ago, long after the development of formal tools such as choppers and hand axes, skeletal remains show a shift in the anatomy of *Homo erectus* that paleoanthropologists describe as 'gracilization', meaning that skeletal remains show males became less robust and closer to females in size. At the same time, archaeological evidence for behaviour reflects more sociality, with camps, regional interactions and more cultural behaviour in general. One archaeological finding stands out particularly; 400,000-year-old javelins, found at the Schöningen site in southern Germany. From our perspective, this was when projectile weaponry killed the alpha male.

It was perhaps inevitable that hominids would develop weaponry that could be used at a distance. This would clearly be effective for hunting prey, as William Calvin (see Chapter 16) has investigated.[92] But projectile weapons would also allow a smaller, less aggressive, non-alpha male to kill from behind or without fear of retaliation from the alpha male victim. The selective advantages of being large and aggressive would rapidly diminish, and those with more social skills, those who could negotiate status rather than create status through bullying, would have a distinct advantage over purely aggressive tactics. This would explain the decreasing physical robustness of males. We now finally see incontrovertible evidence for violence; in the poor individual found at Bodo in Kenya who had been scalped[93] – a clear indication that violence, and the status of trophies, have long evolutionary histories.

But it is not until after 45,000 years ago that we see extensive evidence of violence and warfare. For at about the same time as the development of shared symbols of belief systems, modern humans started formally burying their dead in graves (earlier Neanderthals also did this, as Steven Mithen discusses in Chapter 9, but not to the same extent). This is especially seen at the end of the last Ice Age when, with increasingly sedentary groups, formal cemeteries were developed.

More burials means much more evidence for violence was preserved, for instance at the 12,000 to 14,000-year-old cemetery at Jebel Sahaba on the Upper Nile River, excavated by archaeologist Fred Wendorf and his colleagues.[94] Of the 59 burials at the site, almost half of the individuals died a violent death, indiscriminate of sex or age. Flint points or spear barbs were embedded in limb bones and vertebral columns, and also lay in the abdomens and chest cavities where they had been buried in flesh. Cutmarks on the bones also attest to the violence. Men, women and children were sporadically buried over time but many of the victims had been interred at the same time, indicating that small groups are being killed in single events.

The casualties include nine adult males, nine adult females and three juveniles. The 21 victims were deposited in at least six, and perhaps ten, events resulting in a range of 2.0 to 3.5 deaths per episode, an encounter death rate quite consistent with small-scale societies throughout the world, but an overall death rate higher than most. The 21 victims had a total of 110 projectile points and barbs either embedded in bone or in positions that implied they were a product of conflict. Some were shot many times, others only once. This is not unusual. The concept of overkill is common in all societies, especially when there is status involved or there is a desire to dehumanize the victim. In most hunter-gatherer and village-based societies, anyone who participates in the killing, even if the victim is already dead, gets some credit for participating.

Jebel Sahaba is the first clear example of warfare only because it is the earliest large cemetery preserved in the archaeological record, not because it is the first warfare. This raises questions. Did warfare begin with the rise of fixed territories, as marked by cemeteries, or is violence just more visible in the archaeological record once cemeteries appear? We believe that it is unequivocally the latter, in that cemeteries arose with the rise of more fixed hunting and gathering territories, which just continued a pattern of violence that have been present for thousands of years.

Approximately 7,500 years ago, at the site of Ofnet, Bavaria, a large number of men, women and children were killed and beheaded. Their heads, with cervical vertebrae still attached, were placed in a cave in two adjacent pits. Biological anthropologist David Frayer notes that all of the male skulls have bludgeon wounds that were incurred at the time of death, as do 23 per cent of the females and 59 per cent of the unsexed skulls.[95] Frayer argues that the heads, with their articulated cervical vertebrae, were simultaneously placed in these pits in the aftermath of one incident, a 'massive burial' of a segment of the larger population. The fate of other parts of the bodies is unknown. Outsiders most likely killed the victims, and the heads could very well be trophies, but it seems unlikely that enemies would carefully deflesh and inter the skulls in tidy nests. There are twice as many female victims as male, and three times as many children as adult males, a pattern usually attributed to a strong ethnic or religious bias.

Across the world in north-western Canada, a rare and spectacular case was found at Saunaktuk, in the modern-day Inuit Eskimo-Gwich'in Athabaskan border area.[96] The scattered remains of 35 Inuit women, children and elderly showed evidence of facial mutilation, defleshing of the heads, decapitation, cut muscles, severed joints, split and gouged bones with signs of marrow extraction, and severed hands and feet. Human bones were randomly scattered amidst other animal bones, and both were butchered in the same fashion. Oral tradition places the Inuit men out hunting beluga whales while the (probably) Gwich'in tortured and massacred these families. Dating to approximately AD 1600, this is a clear but terrible example of what one group can do to another when the victims are not considered human by the perpetrators. That foraging societies can be genocidal as effectively as Neolithic, Iron Age or modern peoples radically contradicts Michael Mann's recent argument that these behaviour are strictly a product of modern events.[97]

Some anthropologists see it as rare or unnatural for one group of people to attack another just because they are different[98] but actually, humans are quite adept at classifying other humans as 'other' or even 'non-human,' and then killing them. We are quick and adept at forming groups, treating our own with special favour, and proficiently using aggression on those not in their own group.

Humans are exceptionally good at identifying friends and enemies. These uncomplicated categories fit almost any conditions. The opposing football team is unquestionably an enemy, subject to stereotyping and discrimination. Mascots take all kinds of abuse for their team. Should one player be traded to a favourite team, he automatically becomes a comrade of the new team, and enemy of the old, deserving of support and defence.

In *Demonic Males*, Wrangham and Peterson define this as the 'ingroup–outgroup bias,' a dehumanizing, often ethnocentric, bias that pops up around race, religion, sex, age, sports, grade school, high school and summer camp. It is not a misidentification of those people with strange accents, language, dress and religion as a wholly different (and potentially threatening) species, as Francesco Gil-White argued.[99]

After all, societies most often interact and fight with their nearest neighbours. Many societies such as Iñupiat of North Alaska, New Guinea's Mae Enga and the Tupinamba of Brazil who intermarried, traded within their respective societies, and even allied together, inevitably engaged in war. While the tactical objective among the many arctic societies was to destroy the enemy, these same groups often had the most enduring trade relationships.[100] Memberships shifted back and forth and factions could be allied *and* at war. War and exchange were not mutually exclusive, as they engaged in reciprocal enmity and peace, and allied only for as long as it was necessary. They classified their enemy as the evil out-group in order to win the war. The most successful strategy requires intimidation, dehumanizing and demoralizing the enemy.

Differences between warring peoples are often not perceptible to outsiders, such as between the Hutu and Tutsi of Rwanda or the Serbs and Croats of the Balkans, where ethnic cleansing gruesomely makes this point. That ordinary people commit these violent acts is particularly shocking.[101] Wrangham and Peterson credit 'deindividuation' with how one group could massacre, lynch, rape or torture another. Individual identity blurs into the crowd, judgement is lost, and one becomes part of a pack of wolves with the sole purpose of destroying an enemy.

It is also possible for a society to be considered so alien, so subhuman, that they are not even worthy opponents. Colonizers of America and Australia used sterile terms as 'territorial expansion' and 'Manifest Destiny.'[102] Decentralized societies without recognizable leadership or tactics were considered militarily inept 'barbarians' or 'hordes.' Two superpowers matched with similar weaponry fight 'wars' whereas superpowers perform 'military procedures' or 'police actions' against smaller less equipped forces. If two less sophisticated countries are at war, superpowers implement 'humanitarian missions' in the country they want to see win.

All humans are so good at identifying members of their own group versus other groups, or even spontaneously creating in-groups and out-groups as needs arise, that this trait must have a long evolutionary history. Hand in hand with the evolution of cooperation (see David Sloan Wilson's Chapter 12), the in-group out-group bias is a critical aspect of both chimpanzee and human societies. The past was dangerous and throughout our evolutionary history it was advantageous to know immediately whom one could and could not trust. The resulting evolutionary baggage underlies the class, racial, ethnic and religious problems (the 'isms' if you will) that plague us in modern society.

Religion is a fundamental means by which humans classify in-groups and out-groups, the Us versus Them. Since religion crosses genetic, cultural, ethnic, and national boundaries, it is the inevitable means of self-identification in an increasingly global world where access to media is ever present.

Does religion cause warfare? Certainly not. But religion has clearly been the ultimate facilitator of war, letting large groups of unrelated humans find common cause, motivating them to organize, cooperate and kill at a level never before seen in the entire evolutionary history of humanity. The evolution of aggression between coalitions, beginning over 5 million year ago among our common ancestors with chimpanzees, has built the ability to define an in-group, recognize the 'Other', and go out and kill them. This is now manifested in transnational conflicts often defined, or at least justified, by commonalities of belief.

7 Why we are good: Mirror neurons and the roots of empathy

Gordy Slack

We are good because our biology drives us to be good.

Marco Iacoboni

The problem of altruism has vexed biologists since Darwin, particularly after Richard Dawkins published *The Selfish Gene* in the 1970s. Why do people sacrifice their self-interest, sometimes even their lives, in order to help others? Most straightforward genetic models suggest that such behaviour should be selected against quickly and definitively. But if mirror neuron theorists are right, the advantages of directly understanding others may be so great that they blow the evolutionary costs of occasional self-sacrifice out of the water. What's selected for might be the empathy, the enhanced ability to imitate others, and to understand and feel what they are feeling. Altruism might only be a secondary effect of those other, super-adaptive mirror-neuron-related skills, and not necessarily conveying a selectable evolutionary advantage of its own. Nonetheless, altruism, helping others, being good, are so closely tied to our evolutionary natures that they casts a tint on everything we do.

Recent research in neurobiology would explain empathy as the automatic reaction of a kind of brain cells that work together in what neuroscientists call the mirror neuron system. This system, the scientists who study it say, may be key to understanding the biological underpinnings of human empathy. If true, we care a good deal about other people at least partly because we experience their pains, pleasures, successes and failures in much the same way, and in the same parts of the brain, as we experience our own. We are hard-wired to feel what others experience as if it were happening to us. And in a way, a neurological way, what happens to others *is* happening to us.

'The self and the other are just two sides of the same coin. To understand myself, I must recognize myself in other people', Marco Iacoboni explained to me. Iacoboni is not an Eastern mystic; he's a neuroscientist and professor of psychiatry at UCLA, where he directs the Transcranial Magnetic Stimulation Lab at the Ahmanson Lovelace Brain Mapping Center. He refers to a network composed of ordinary-looking neurons concentrated in the brain's premotor cortex and the inferior parietal cortex. Unlike other brain cells, these cells, mirror neurons, fire both when a person does something and when he observes someone else doing that same thing.

When I see a woman on a train wiping her tear-stained cheek, and I wipe my own face as her pain becomes my pain, it's because some of the very same cells in my brain fire from watching her, despite the fact that I am sitting perfectly still. And the neural mirroring going on is not restricted to movement-related neurons; it also occurs in those parts of my brain where emotional responses reside. I mirror not only the woman's face wiping, but also her hopelessness, her desperation, her sadness. She is crying, so to speak, in the same part of my brain where I do. The neurologist Vilayanur Ramachandran calls them 'mind-reading' neurons, 'but without telepathy'. Ramachandran is the director of the Center for Brain and Cognition at the University of California at San Diego: 'We used to say, metaphorically, that "I can feel another's pain". But now we know that my mirror neurons can *literally* feel your pain'.

Enthusiasm for mirror neurons' explanatory powers has gained momentum in the past few years as dozens of published studies have linked them to language, imitation, autism and empathy. If Ramachandran, Iacoboni and the hundreds of other neuroscientists now pouring over mirror neurons are correct, directly sharing the experience of others, what mirror theorists call 'embodied simulation,' is key to who and what we are, how our brains and minds evolved, and how they develop from childhood. Empathy, feeling the experience of another, the neuroscientists are saying, is not just something we're capable of; it is woven into the very fabric we are cut from. And it makes sense of some of our most cherished and essentially human behaviour.

Some of science's biggest discoveries are accidental. In 1963, physicists Arno Penzias and Robert Wilson discovered the first direct evidence of the Big Bang while looking for the source of static-like buzzing coming from their giant radio antenna. After chasing the resident pigeons out of the thing, and sweeping out their droppings, Penzias and Wilson realized that the source of the sound was something much, much bigger: the low-level background radiation Big Bang advocates had predicted astronomers would eventually find evenly distributed all over the Universe. In 1973, the two physicists won the Nobel Prize for their serendipitous discovery.

In the early 1990s, neuroscientist Giacomo Rizzolatti and his research team at the University of Parma sort of tripped over mirror neurons, too. They were studying motor neurons in the frontal cortex of macaques and had attached tiny electrodes to individual cells in the monkeys so they could watch how very specific hand movements were initiated in the brain. When a wired-up monkey picked up a peanut, the neuron fired. But to Rizzolatti's surprise, the same motor neuron also fired when a perfectly still monkey was watching a lab assistant pick up the peanut. Why would a motor neuron fire, Rizzolatti asked, when there was no motor action? Many tests, retests and innovations on the retests later revealed the whole new class of brain cells: mirror neurons.

When Rizzolatti's research was published in 1992[103] the neuroscience community went ape looking for evidence of mirror neurons in other primates and in humans. Because it is unethical and illegal to go fishing with electrodes into human brains, scientists had to search with other, less invasive tools. The functional magnetic resonance imaging (fMRI) revolution in neuroscience was under way, allowing scientists to observe accurate, high-resolution, three-dimensional images of brain activity in real time (see Andrew Newberg's Chapter 11). Neurobiologists looked for mirror-like brain activity in the same areas where the systems had been found in macaques. And they found evidence of them in far greater numbers and more elaborate formulations than in macaques or any other primates.

Humans are 'heavily wired' with mirror neurons, according to Ramachandran, but only very recently have scientists identified individual mirror neurons in humans. Iacoboni's team at UCLA collaborated with Itzhak Fried, a neurosurgeon who was implanting electrodes into epileptic patients in an effort to find the origins of their seizures so they could be surgically treated. Once those electrodes were in place, and after patients gave permission, it was possible for Iacoboni to test individual human neurons for mirroring. He found mirror neurons in several locations. Their recent report[104] made a splash in the scientific community, but it only confirmed what neurologists had been observing indirectly through fMRI for several years.

The evolutionary roots of human mirror neuron systems reach back millions of years, according to Michael Arbib, Director of the USC Brain Project and author of *From Action to Language via the Mirror System*. The evolution of language appears to be connected to the mirror-neuron-rich area of the brain associated with movements of the hands, he says, while the evolution of our empathic emotion mirroring capabilities seem to be associated with regions of the brain associated with movements in the face.

Early mirroring must have enhanced our ancestors' ability to learn by imitation – one primate can 'practise' using tools in its head simply by watching another. These new capacities eventually led to the kind of 'metaphorical' exercises employed in abstraction of all kinds, including the development of symbolic systems like language, says Ramachandran, whose lab at UCSD is currently investigating the connection between mirror neurons and the human ability to employ metaphor. 'Not just literary metaphors,' Ramachandran told me, 'but abstractions of all kinds. Once you understand the cross-modal computations that mirror neurons are doing, you can see why human beings are so good at all kinds of abstraction.'

Other primates engage in 'cross-modal abstraction,' or metaphor, too, according to Ramachandran, but humans are qualitatively distinct even from the most speculative and metaphorical apes. Some millions of years ago, the part of the mammalian brain in the left inferior parietal lobule mushroomed. This mirror-neuron-rich area, called the angular gyrus, is far more developed in humans than in other primates. And when the angular gyrus is damaged, Ramachandran finds that patients experience metaphor blindness. Ramachandran argues that being able to make abstractions – to go from recognition of a vertical limb, say, to the abstract notion of verticality, and then to assign it a word, 'verticality,' or eventually a mathematical representation with which you can work abstractly from the limb itself, conveys a clear evolutionary advantage.

What sets humans apart is not just, or even mostly, modelling trees or weather or other inanimate things. It's modelling each other. Other kinds of animals can imitate one another, but only primates as far as we know have the mirror neuron systems necessary to actually feel each other's pain or know each other's intentions, according to Ramachandran. For humans, failure to internalize others leads to serious disabilities. Autism, according to Iacoboni, may result from a breakdown or suppression of the mirror system, rendering those afflicted with the condition less empathic, worse at reading the emotional states of others, and less emotionally connected to those around them. Iacoboni finds that autistics show significantly less mirror neuron activity.

The ability to model what others are thinking was a key evolutionary innovation, Steven Mithen (see Chapter 9) and many others have argued.[105] Theory of mind, as neuroscientists and anthropologists call this capacity, made it possible for our hominid ancestors to live in social groups. Ramachandran has speculated that the evolution of the self evolved not first to give each person a conscious foreman, but as a way to model others. In Ramachandran's mirror-neuron-related explanation, the self began as a kind of a little modelling programme – fed with data from the mirror system – for understanding other people, a kind of algorithm for generating a mini-you in me, he told me.

Once it evolved, this modelling programme turned around and began to apply its algorithmic investigations also to its host, the brain in which it resided. Self-consciousness was born. 'It was almost certainly a two-way street,' Ramachandran said, 'with self-awareness and other-awareness enriching each other in an auto-catalytic cascade that culminated in the fully human sense of self. For example, you say you are being "self-conscious" when you really mean being conscious of someone else being conscious of you.'

The mirror neuron craze has its critics – among them is UC Berkeley developmental psychologist Alison Gopnik, who calls mirror neurons a 'myth' and says their power to explain consciousness, language and empathy is purely metaphorical. Tufts University Philosopher Daniel Dennett agrees that it is too soon to draw profound conclusions about the role of mirror neurons. Dennett, director of the Center for Cognitive Studies Tufts University and the author of *Darwin's Dangerous Idea* (1996), says that 'some mirror neuron enthusiasts are saying that these are some kind of magic bullet, a giant leap by evolution that made language and empathy possible. I think that is much too strong.'

Ramachandran and Dennett, who are friends, just disagree on this point. The UC San Diego neuroscientist thinks that mirror neurons will indeed bring about a revolution in the way we see the brain, the way we see ourselves, and our relationship to one another. 'Mirror neurons will do for psychology what the discovery of DNA did for biology,' Ramachandran wrote in a now famous essay.[106]

Whoever is right, it is certainly worth asking what it would mean to science, to religion, and to the modern culture in which they both reside, if the mirror neuron enthusiasts are correct. What if compassion, empathy and the human longing for justice – not to mention the emergence of language and the ability to engage in abstract reasoning and to employ metaphor – all stem from one historical turn in the evolution of the human brain? In that case, our connection to others wouldn't be just one feature of the human brain (and mind) but rather an essential and defining one. Perhaps even *the* defining feature, the secret to our success as a species and the key to understanding how we interact.

Before the discovery of mirror neurons, most cognitive scientists assumed that we understood each other by figuring one another out. You would see a person crying on the train, say, and you would draw a set of logical inferences from that about what she was feeling and doing. You would then flesh those out by comparing them to times when you did and felt similar things and then assign an emotional flavouring based on your conclusions. In contrast, the mirror system allows a simple, direct experience to replace much of that computation, speculation and inference.

Iacoboni quotes Ludwig Wittgenstein, who, in his *Remarks on the Philosophy of Psychology*, wrote: 'We see emotion. . . . We do not see facial contortions and make the inference that [someone] is feeling joy, grief, boredom. We describe a face immediately as sad, radiant, bored'. Of course Wittgenstein knew nothing of mirror neurons, but Iacoboni sees his observation as exactly right, in that we experience others' emotions directly.

According to Ramachandran, while mirror neurons may 'dissolve the barrier between you and someone else,' they wouldn't be of much use if we could not *reconstruct* that barrier somehow, if we could not tell the difference between ourselves and others. Ramachandran speculates that there must be other circuitry that inhibits that barrier-breaking empathic response, so a nurse doesn't cry out each time she sticks a syringe into a child's arm.

Recent research by Iacoboni and his colleagues bears out Ramachandran's prediction.[107] The UCLA study found that, while some mirror neurons increase their firing when an action is being observed, others nearby decrease theirs. The excited neurons are creating the sensation of another's experience, while the suppressed ones are telling their host that that pain belongs to someone else. When damage occurs to the parts of the brain that apply such inhibition, patients may be unable to control the urge to mimic others. And patients whose mirror neurons do not self-identify may be unable to distinguish between someone else's actions and their own. Echolalia, whose victims compulsively repeat whatever is said to them, is one well-documented dysfunction of this kind. Ramachandran speculates that kinds of schizophrenia may also be the result of a breakdown in the mirror-system-related ability to distinguish self from other, model from experience, reality from imagination.

The questions Iacoboni and Ramahandran address in their daily research are ones historically reserved for philosophers and theologians: What are minds? What is the relationship between the physical world of the brain and the experiential and psychological world of the mind? What is the self, and how is it related to the rest of the world? How do we learn about the world? How can we ever validate what we think we know? How does language work? How do we gain access to the truth? What is the ground of ethics?

In addressing these questions, neurobiology will surely influence the philosophical and theological approaches we've been wrestling with for centuries. Neuroscience doesn't just address the question of our place in the Universe (as Galileo did) or how we got here (as Darwin did) – though brain science will have plenty to say about both those things, too – it also gets at the essence of our experience itself, how we know others, why we have selves, why we desire what we do, believe what we do, do what we do. If Ramachandran is right and human self consciousness – perhaps the crowning achievement of human evolution – has its roots in the evolutionary innovation marked by our ancestors' efforts to feel each others' pains and pleasures, to know each others' minds, then it is no wonder we have such a capacity for so-called selflessness, for compassion, for doing good.

Ramachandran calls the mirror neurons at the root of empathy, 'Gandhi neurons', but understanding someone else, or even feeling their pain, doesn't always result in kindness or compassion. Maybe not even half the time. Mirror neurons may help you read the minds and emotions of others, but what you do with that knowledge is going to be influenced by the decision-making frontal cortex, according to Ramachandran. A boxer may be able to feel his opponent's pain, take that insight, and then hit him again in exactly the same spot. So, while mirror neurons may explain why we have such a great capacity for being very good indeed, the insider knowledge they convey may also explain why we can be so accomplished, too, when it comes to being horrid: our ability to 'know thy enemy'.

While mirror neurons may explain the direct emotional impact a crying stranger on a train has on me, they don't explain why I may do nothing to help her. We are interconnected, yes, maybe fundamentally so, but we are still individuals, too. So perhaps, as Gopnik says, the leap that connects the co-firing of neurons to the human condition is only a metaphor after all. But then, Ramachandran points out, a good mirror-neuron-enabled metaphor is itself one of the most powerful things a human can have. Or share. And if the interconnectedness of people becomes a dominant metaphor for the 21st century that, I suspect, will bolster our chances of persisting to the 22nd by a great deal. And if they could see it, that metaphor would surely please our favourite sages – theists, deists and atheists alike – from the Buddha, Gandhi, and Jesus to Einstein, Darwin and Spinoza.

8 The evolution of religion

Lewis Wolpert

I believe that religion and mystical thinking arose from these causal beliefs as our ancestors wanted to know the causes of events that affected their lives. Humans have a basic need to construct beliefs that account for important events in their lives, and religion provides some of the basic explanations. This cognitive imperative evolved because it was an evolutionary advantage for human survival to have causal beliefs that led tool making. As Tim Taylor discusses in Chapter 10, it was technology that drove human evolution, and humans may be distinguished from all other animals in having beliefs about the causal interaction of physical objects.

As I discussed in my recent book, *Six Impossible Things Before Breakfast,*[108] the word *belief* is not easy to define. A characteristic of belief, unlike common knowledge is that it always graded with respect to our confidence in it: it has a true and false value, how right or wrong it is. One can think of causal belief as an explanatory tool for understanding the physical world and it is programmed into our brains.[109]

Causal understanding in children is a developmental primitive.[110] From 3 months, infants can apparently reason about physical causality. They reason about these events according to three principles, which may be genetically determined: (1) moving objects maintain both connectedness and cohesion, that is they do not break up or fuse; (2) objects move continuously, and they do not disappear and appear again without other objects in the way; and (3) they move together or interact only if they touch. There are many experiments to support this – for example, infants clearly understand that for a moving block to make another one move, it must make contact with it. At an early age, children know that a moving object – a ball – can make another move on impact. It is this primitive concept of mechanics, which may be the key causal belief, which originally evolved in early humans. At 18 months they are effectively using objects as tools. Children ask many questions about causes.

Animals, in contrast, have very limited causal beliefs though they can learn to carry out complex tasks. According to psychologist Michael Tomasello,[111] humans, unlike all other primates, can understand causal and intentional relations concerning external entities. One may illustrate the differences in chimpanzee and human thinking with the claim that non-human primates, seeing the wind blowing and shaking a branch till the fruit falls, would never believe, from this, that they could shake the branch to get the fruit.

One might have thought that Wolfgang Kohler's experiments with chimpanzees showed just the opposite. His chimpanzees, some 80 years ago, could sometimes, perhaps with some training, stack boxes on top of each other to get a banana nailed to the ceiling. But Kohler himself acknowledged that the chimpanzees had no knowledge of the forces involved. For example, they would try to place one box on another along its diagonal edge; and if stones were placed on the ground so that the box toppled over, they never removed the stones.

Chimpanzees and apes are thus at the edge of causal understanding as shown by their use of simple tools, such as using a stone to break nuts, or trimming a grass reed to get out ants. But in no case of stone tool use is there evidence of modifying the structure of the stone to improve its function.

The studies of Daniel Povinelli,[112] a behavioural biologist, have shown that apes, for example, cannot select an appropriate tool for a simple physical manipulation without training. Nevertheless, tamarin monkeys are able to correctly choose the right simple tool to get food, and biological anthropologist Marc Hauser[113] has found that tamarin monkeys choose to pull on a scarf that has the reward on it, rather than one just close to it. New Caledonian crows manufacture and use several types of tools for getting at insects and other invertebrates, including straight and hooked sticks, and complex stepped-cut flat tools made from leaves.[114] So while animals like crows and some primates have some understanding of tool use, they have a very limited capacity for refining and combining objects to make better tools.

The evolutionary advantage of causal beliefs in humans is related to the making and use of tools, both simple and complex. One cannot make a mildly complex tool without a concept of cause and effect. By 'complex' I mean a tool that has a well-characterized form for the use to which it will be put and, even more importantly, any tool made out of two pieces put together, like a spear with a stone head. It is only with causal beliefs that technology became possible, and it was technology – the ability to physically interact with the environment – that made life easier. Just consider things as apparently as simple as a knife, a basket and the wheel.

Charles Darwin was insistent that chimpanzees, who use sticks to get ants, for example, held mental skills on a continuum with humans. But Darwin eventually conceded to George Douglas Campbell, the Duke of Argyll, who claimed that 'the fashioning of an implement for a special purpose is absolutely peculiar to humans'. With *Man the Tool-Maker,*[115] anthropologist Kenneth Oakley later made clear that humans can be distinguished as the only tool-making primate. Only humans effectively cause one object to interact with another (or with the environment) in a multitude of different ways.

Humans invented technology, which effectively drove human evolution, as Tim Taylor discusses in Chapter 10, and as Steven Mithen discusses in Chapter 9, there is even evidence that specific regions of the human brain are associated with tool use. A key component of this ability has been suggested to be a causal operator in the brain, which may involve connections between the left frontal lobe and left orientation area. There is evidence from brain imaging studies that distinct brain regions are related to knowledge about different classes of objects, such as people, plants and tools.[116] Patients with strokes who have damage to these areas have great difficulty with causal thinking and often do not know why something happened.

As archaeologists Taylor and Mithen discuss, the first stone tools were essentially flaked and smashed-up quartz pebbles, and the first known stone tool industry consisted of simple stone flakes. Even for a modern human it requires several hours to master. A carefully controlled sharp glancing blow is required to initiate a fracture in making the tool and requires a concept of cause and effect. It took at least a million years to go from the stone axes to other and more complex tools. By some 300,000 years ago, tool-making skills had accelerated and by the Middle Stone Age there is clear evidence of hafted tools, that is they are composites, with the components joined together.[117] This was a major advance since one clearly cannot make such a tool – joining quite different pieces together – without having a very clear concept of cause and effect. About 20,000 years ago, bows and arrows make their appearance together with needles and sewing. Moreover some of the tools were no longer merely extensions of common bodily movements. A hammer is essentially a weighted fist and using a saw involves recognizing a quite new causal principle.

Contrary to the emphasis that others and I have given to tool use in human evolution, there is quite a widely held view that primate brain evolution has been driven principally by the demands of the social world rather than by the demands of interacting with the physical environment. The evolutionary anthropologist Robin Dunbar[118] claims that primate brain evolution has been driven principally by the demands of the social world, particularly with other members of the group. He argues that human brain growth, language and intelligent behaviour were evolutionary changes related to the increasing social complexity of community life among hominids (pre-human ancestors). For Dunbar, the evolution of language enabled cooperation between hominids needed for larger social groups to bond together. But without causal thinking about interactions of objects, I find it hard to see how improved social understanding could have been a real advantage, or how it could have led to technology.

Religious beliefs are universal, complex and variable, and present a difficult problem when considering how they originated, are acquired and modified. My suggestion, similar to that of Tim Taylor, is that they all had their origin in the evolution of causal beliefs, which in turn had its origins in tool use, through the evolutionary advantage these beliefs provided for making and using more complex tools. Given causal beliefs it was natural for our ancestors to ask 'Why' questions about life and death. One needs to consider the life style of the earliest humans. They were hunter-gatherers, and group activity and tool use were very important.

A key proposal I wish to put forward[119] is that once causal belief evolved in relation to tools, and language evolved, it was inevitable that people would want to understand the causes of all the events that affected their lives from illness, through changes in climate, to death itself. Once there was a concept of cause and effect, ignorance was no longer bliss, and this could have led to religious beliefs. People wanted to know what caused the important events in their lives, what would happen in the future and what action they should take. Uncertainty about major issues that affected their lives was as intolerable then as it is now. Religion provided causal understanding. Humans were the most obvious causal agents. Religion also offered the possibility of asking for help by praying.

Foremost, our ancestors wanted to know the causes of 'evil' and incomprehensible events. The one causative agent that our ancestors were sure about was their own and other peoples' actions, particularly those learned from tool making and altering the environment. They are the most clear-cut examples of causes and led to belief in human-like gods.

For many religions, there is a belief in a God who is like a person without a normal body, free, eternal, all knowing and capable of doing anything. There are very few societies without religious beliefs, which strongly supports the idea that it had an evolutionary advantage. Religious beliefs were adaptive for two main reasons: they provided explanations for important events and also offered prayer as a way of dealing with difficulties.

Since causal beliefs that promote survival are partly programmed by our genes, could that not also be true of some aspects of religious beliefs that promote survival, particularly those that relate to mystical forces and even, perhaps to the gods themselves? Religious beliefs provided gods or ancestors who could be prayed to, and who might help to solve problems. Those with such beliefs may have been better adapted for survival if they were less anxious and healthier.

What is the relationship between religion and health? If it is positive, then religion could be an adaptive in evolution. Although the studies should be regarded as tentative, the evidence is that there is an inverse relationship between pain intensity, and religious beliefs.[120] This is consistent with the findings that those within a religious community enjoy better mental health, possible due to social support. There is also evidence that religious activities reduce psychological stress and promote greater well-being and optimism, and so help to reduce the bodily effects of stress such as that on the heart.

Thus those with such beliefs most likely did better, and so were selected for. Religion may thus have evolved to be deep rooted in our biology. Has, then, religious belief a genetic component? The Minnesota twin study did find that there was a genetic influence on whether an individual developed religious beliefs – the heritability was around 50 per cent, which implies a significant genetic component. Almost every culture has a belief in a spiritual world that contains a god who can be prayed to and is in control of powerful forces.

One model proposes that activation of the autonomic nervous system – the one which is not directly under our control and which controls our heart rate and blood flow, for example – acts on those regions of the brain responsible for mental experience, such as the temporal lobes. These lobes are thought to modulate feelings and emotions. Evidence for a role of the temporal lobes in religious experience comes from epilepsy originating in these lobes, and their association with sudden religious conversions. It is suggested that the visions of St. Teresa may have been associated with temporal lobe epilepsy.

It is thus of great interest that Michael Pensinger has stimulated the brains of subjects with electromagnets which causes tiny seizures in the temporal lobes. Many subjects had supernatural spiritual experiences, even religious ones, which included the sense of something or someone else in the room, distortion of their bodies and religious feelings.

Religion is concerned with the supernatural, and thus involves forces and causes beyond our normal experience of nature, and this is something we need to understand. Humans will perhaps seek rewards through the supernatural if they are not obtainable by other means. In considering what makes religious beliefs seem so natural to many people, Pascal Boyer[121] rejects the view that it is just people's wish to deal with misfortune or understand the Universe. For Boyer, it involves a complex variety of mental processes used to account for evil events, with religion as a product of the supernatural imagination, which in turn involves counterintuitive notions.

A large number of people hold paranormal beliefs that invoke forces and causes both outside ordinary experience and science, they offer believers new powers. It is also not unreasonable to think that some religious beliefs are paranormal – consider Christ's miracles, his rising from the dead and the supposed effectiveness of prayer. Paranormal beliefs may partly be the result of trying to explain events for which no simple explanation seems possible, together with a preference for invoking mystical causes and forces (Robert Layton similarly discusses Aboriginal cosmology in Chapter 3, and William Calvin mentions shamans in Chapter 16). Some 3 per cent of Americans believe in ghosts, 70 per cent in angels, and as many as one in ten has claimed to have seen, or had contact with, a ghost. These experiences include not just ghostly apparitions but unusual smells, and the strong sense of someone or something being present. In addition, 25 per cent claim to have had a telepathic experience, and 11 per cent had seen a flying saucer. Around 50 per cent of the population believed in extrasensory perception.

I suggest that our brains are programmed for such beliefs. This genetic contribution may have programmed our brains to have spiritual and paranormal experiences easily. When viewed in this way, hallucinations and delusions may reflect a basic programme in the brain that, for a variety of reasons, could be activated at inappropriate times. Thus religious experiences may have become linked to paranormal beliefs, delusions and hallucinations. Consider this statement by Timothy Leary after he had taken LSD: 'I discovered that beauty, revelation, sensuality, the cellular history of the past, God, the Devil – all lie inside my body, outside my mind'. How could LSD, a rather simple molecule, induce such experiences if the circuits in the brain for such experiences are not already there?

Michael Schumaker refers to the 'paranormal belief imperative'. He argues that we are pre-eminently auto-hypnotic creatures and suggests that humans being are 'A believing phenomenon, who must believe in order to live at all'. Similarly, Lucien Lévy Bruhl, a French anthropologist of the early 20th century, made this connection: 'There is a mystical mentality more marked and more easily observable among primitive societies than our own, but present in every human mind. That is a sense of an invisible power and a reality other than our normal reality. It is something fundamental and indestructible in human nature.' Further evidence for this comes from studies on groups given the active ingredient of magic mushrooms, psilocybin, can cause mystical and religious experiences, which implies that such circuits are in our brains. There may thus be some genetic tendency to have mystical and religious beliefs.[122]

A rather different approach to the evolution of religious beliefs emphasizes the social aspects of belonging to a religious community, and the extent this brings advantages to the members. David Sloan Wilson looks at human society as an organism in its own right, and thus at the evolution of society in Darwinian terms. I see this approach as somewhat flawed, since there is no way in which a society, religious or not, conforms with the evolution of organisms, as there is nothing equivalent to replication of the genes or their programming of the behaviour of the organism in a society.

In his recent book, *Darwin's Cathedral*,[123] Wilson attempts to understand a religious community in its relation to its environment from an evolutionary perspective, and focuses on John Calvin's views of Christianity in Geneva in the 16th century. How adaptive, he asks, was Calvinism for the inhabitants of Geneva? Calvin placed equal emphasis on people's relationship with God and on their relationship with other people, duties of charity that were owed to one's neighbours. Calvinism included, of course, the Ten Commandments, which may help societies to have adaptive belief systems which lead to behaviour similar to cooperation with one's neighbours. Again the system must cope with the problem of some individuals exploiting others' good behaviour.

But it remains far from clear in what evolutionary sense Calvin's society was adaptive in the evolutionary sense of ensuring reproduction and survival of its citizens. Its administration may have been very fair, and individuals may have liked many aspects of it, but from evolution's viewpoint this is irrelevant, since only reproductive advantage matters. The Balinese goddess who helps with water irrigation of the rice fields, and ensures cooperation in the distribution of the water, provides a better example. This coordinates the activities of thousands of farmers for their mutual benefit. In the light of this thinking, Wilson suggests it is plausible to argue that we are genetically programmed to have a psychology sympathetic to the adaptive rules of religion.

9 Is religion inevitable? An archaeologist's view from the past

Steven Mithen

Our species, *Homo sapiens*, is a product of biological evolution that has conditioned the manner in which we think. As far as we can ascertain, the capacity for religious thought is not present within the chimpanzee, our closest living relative with which we shared a common ancestor 5–6 million years ago. As a consequence, this capacity must have arisen since the divergence between the chimpanzee and human lineages. This does not necessarily imply that a 'capacity for religious thought' exists as a discrete entity within the mind and was specifically selected for during human evolution, as is likely to be the case for capacities such as theory of mind and language. That for religion might simply be the consequence of other selected cognitive traits that when combined together provide humans with this unique manner of thought.

The span of 6 million years provides a vast expanse of time during which religious thought may have emerged. It could be an attribute of all members of the *Homo* genus, hence appearing prior to 2 million years ago. Alternatively, it might depend upon the possession of brains of a size beyond some threshold, perhaps not appearing until, say, 500,000 years ago and hence be an attribute of large brained hominins such as *Homo heidelbergensis, neanderthalensis* and *sapiens*, leaving smaller brained hominins such as *Homo habilis* without religion. Other possibilities are that religious thought is a unique attribute of either all members of *Homo sapiens*, or only those after particular social and economic conditions had arisen, such as communities of a particular size and structure. The latter would require there to be a particular conjunction of biological traits and cultural conditions before the capacity for religious thought emerged.

The easy task is to come up with theories as to when, how and why a capacity for religious belief arose during the course of human evolution, in the manner of, say, Pascal Boyer,[124] Lewis Wolpert[125] and Daniel Dennett.[126] The more challenging, and more interesting, task to find means to evaluate such theories against the archaeological record. Hence this essay will primarily focus on some of the methodological challenges archaeologists face when seeking to identify whether religious thought was present in past societies and what its characteristics might have been. I will, however, indulge myself towards its conclusion with my own particular theory as to when, why and how religion evolved, and one that suggests that religion has indeed been inevitable within human society ever since the origin of *Homo sapiens* and will always remain so.

What is religion?

Before embarking on this task I ought to attempt some form of definition. In general terms, I am simply referring to belief in supernatural agency, whether that is defined as belief in one God, many Gods, spirits, ghosts, animism and so forth. Pascal Boyer[127] has usefully re-defined God as an 'all-knowing strategic agent', while I also include the attribution of knowledge, will and purpose to inanimate entities as a key element of religious thought. I find the distinction that Harvey Whitehouse[128] has drawn between 'imagistic' and 'doctrinal' modes of religiosity useful, especially as these can be broadly related to forms of socio-economic organization. According to Whitehouse, the imagistic mode consists of the tendency within certain small scale or regionally fragmented ritual traditions and cults for revelation to be transmitted through sporadic collective action, evoking multivocal iconic imagery, encoded in memory as distinct episodes, and producing highly cohesive and particularistic social ties. In contrast, the doctrinal mode of religiosity consists of the tendency within many regional and world religions for revelations to be codified as a body of doctrine, transmitted through routinized forms of worship, memorized as part of one's general knowledge and a product of large, anonymous communities.

The recognition of either mode of religiosity from archaeological evidence provides many challenges. The doctrinal mode is more accessible as this tends to create monumental architecture and iconic symbols shared over an extensive area, although identifying these as necessarily of a religious nature may not be as easy as it may initially appear. Moreover, as the doctrinal mode of religiosity is likely to be derivative of a state scale of social organization of the type that only originated after 5,000 years ago, prehistorians are predominately concerned with identifying religious activity that would fall within Whitehouse's imagistic mode.

Four archaeological challenges

The most systematic attempt to develop an explicit methodology was by Colin Renfrew in his 1985 book, *The Archaeology of Cult.*[129] This exposed the many steps of inference that an archaeologist must go through when seeking to identify religious activity, often involving the elimination of other explanations for the presence of particular types of artefacts and their particular spatial location and associations within a settlement.

Of the numerous methodological challenges involved in the identification of religious activity from the archaeological record, four can be briefly considered. First, religious thought may have no material representation – it may reside entirely within the mind of an individual. While this cannot be entirely ruled out, I argue below that this is highly unlikely as material objects are frequently, perhaps always, required as cognitive anchors for religious ideas that do not sit comfortably within an evolved mind. There remains a dilemma, however, as those material objects might be entirely natural, such as a mountain top or an unmodified stone. As such, although they are visible, an archaeologist is unlikely to appreciate their significance.

Second, religious belief may have material representation but this may be of a nature that does not survive in the archaeological record. All of the objects and structures involved in religious activity might be made from organic materials and hence subject to rapid decay. While this will always be one of the fundamental problems with the reconstruction of past activity and thought, some aspects of it are being alleviated by the developments in archaeological science that continue to enhance the recovery of evidence. The development of isotopic studies of human bone, for instance, has provided archaeologists with information about past diet when no food remains have been preserved while micro-morphological studies of floor deposits have extracted unprecedented amounts of information about past activities. Both of these can be used to enhance our understanding of past religion, such as by identifying individuals who may have had special diets and areas where non-domestic activities occurred.

A third problem is simply the ambiguity of so much archaeological evidence: objects and structures can be easily misinterpreted as being of religious nature; conversely, items of a religious significance may not be recognized as such – a manger in a stable is likely to be interpreted simply as a feeding place for cattle. A classic example of the former is Neanderthal burial.[130] The discovery that some Neanderthal bodies, of both adults and infants, had been carefully laid within shallow pits inevitably led to proposals about beliefs in an afterlife, while objects found within those so-called graves, such as stone artefacts, animal bones and remnants from flowers, were interpreted as the consequence of graveside ritual. But such burials might be no more than the disposal of 'rubbish' in a reasonably hygienic manner and all such artefacts may be part of the rubbish or present for entirely unrelated reasons, such as the parts of flowers coming from the burrowing of rodents – as is likely in the (in)famous case of the Shanidar Neanderthal burials.

A fourth problem to note (there are numerous others, but describing them all will make this essay too depressing) is that our definition of religion might be too restrictive. This derives from the present-day world, or at least that of the recent historical past, which provides us with just a small fraction of the human communities that have lived since the *Homo* genus appeared more than 2 million years ago. It may be the case that forms of religious belief and action existed in the past that have no modern equivalence; by defining religion on the basis of what we know today, as in the manner of Whitehouse, we risk becoming blind to that of the past.

Three archaeological examples

It will be useful here to provide three brief examples from specific archaeological sites that illustrate these problems and the dilemmas that archaeologists face when interpreting the material they excavate.

Blombos Cave, on the western cape of South Africa is one of the most important sites currently being excavated as it provides some of the earliest evidence for symbolic behaviour. In deposits dating to at least 70,000 years old, shell beads and numerous fragments of incised ochre have been found, some of which have undisputed geometric designs.[131] These have been interpreted as the earliest evidence for art, symbolism and even language. It is almost irresistible to interpret such objects in this manner, especially when they have been found with other objects typical of symbol-using modern humans, such as bone points and elegant stone points. Red pigment is also abundant in the cave, suggestive of body painting as widely used in ritual activities by recent San groups. It would, indeed, be contrary to interpret the materials from Blombos cave as indicating anything other than artistic, symbolic, language using humans. This is especially the case as very soon after 70,000 years ago there is a major pulse of human dispersal into Asia and then Europe – another indicator of 'modern' behaviour. But the question we face is whether those artefacts from Blombos also imply religious humans, presumably of the 'imagistic mode': did those people who wore shell beads and incised plaques of ochre at Blombos also believe in supernatural beings?

For a second example we can consider one of my own excavations, that of the early Neolithic site of WF16 in southern Jordan.[132] This dates to between 11,500 and 10,200 years ago, the period of the transition from hunting and gathering to farming – arguably the most significant event of the whole of human history. This occurs long after the origin and dispersal of *Homo sapiens* from Africa and we can reasonably assume that the capacity for religious belief was present within the Neolithic people. So at sites such as WF16, we are primarily concerned with trying to identify the particular character of such belief at a specific site or more generally within a cultural period. The burials at this WF16 provide some of the most compelling evidence for religion.

One of these involved a single inhumation within a circular stone structure in which the head of the deceased was partially detached from the body and laid upon a stone 'pillow'. The cranium appears to have protruded through the floor and hence was visible to those undertaking whatever activities occurred within the structure, these including an extensive use of stone points probably for working reeds and leather. A burial within another structure is similar in terms of being close to where seemingly domestic activities had taken place, in this case a quern used for grinding plant material. This burial also had a skull carefully placed on a pillow stone, but it contained the bones from many individuals, the grave having been frequently opened and closed to add and remove bones during the period of site occupation. Such evidence, along with that from contemporary sites, suggests that 'ancestor worship' (an admittedly inadequate phrase) had been a key element of the Neolithic religious belief and that boundaries between the living and the dead were more fluid than we believe they are today.

Other lines of evidence from WF16 are more difficult to interpret. There are, for instance, numerous pieces of incised stone, part of a stone figurine and a stone phallus – whether these had any religious significance is unclear. The latter is perhaps the most interesting object in light of previous claims about 'fertility cults' and 'mother goddesses' at the origins of agriculture. These views are gradually being overturned by the increasing recognition of 'male' imagery in the early Neolithic, as illustrated by this stone phallus. My own view is that several of the stone pestles from WF16 were made in a deliberately ambiguous fashion to also appear as phalli, relating to a metaphorical association between plant preparation and sexual activity[133] – but whether this should be described as an element of Neolithic religiosity remains unclear to me. More generally, I am uncertain as to where my own boundary between objective inference and subjective speculation resides when I am interpreting the material from WF16 with regard to religious belief (or indeed any form of behaviour and thought). If I cannot define that boundary for one of my own excavations, for a site which I know in its most intimate detail, then can I reliably interpret the material from elsewhere?

For a third example we can look at another of my own excavations, that at the site of Fiskary Bay on the Isle of Coll, Western Scotland.[134] This dates to about 9,000 years ago and is a site of Mesolithic hunter-gatherers. My excavations have so far recovered stone artefacts, charred plant material and fish bones, the latter being of particular interest as the site is close to a relatively recent (probably 17th century) fish trap which may, therefore, have a prehistoric antecedent. There is nothing within the excavated materials that necessarily implies religious behaviour or thought; indeed there is nothing that implies art, symbolism or language.

I have in fact excavated numerous sites of this period within Western Scotland over the last 20 years.[135] When combined with the evidence recovered by other archaeologists in the same region, this work has been able to reconstruct some aspects of the Mesolithic lifestyle in terms of settlement and subsistence activity. But no evidence has been recovered from any site of this period in Western Scotland that unambiguously suggests religious behaviour. In fact, I can't even think of any ambiguous evidence, except for a few pieces of human bone deposited in a shell midden on the island or Oronsay, although this may simply be another case of rubbish disposal.

The most likely reason is simply one of preservations: other than in exceptional circumstances organic remains have been destroyed by the acidic soils and hence we lack human burials and have very few artefacts made from bone, wood, antler. In spite of a complete lack of evidence, it would be bizarre to think that these modern human hunter-gatherers did not have beliefs about supernatural agency. It is far more reasonable to think that they invested the hills, rivers, lochs and woodlands with symbolic meanings – a Mesolithic equivalent of the Dreamtime of the Australian Aborigines. But we have no evidence that this was the case.

The examples of Blombos cave, WF16 and Fiskary Bay, together with that of Neanderthal burial noted above, illustrate some of the problems archaeologists face when seeking to infer both the existence of religious belief and its specific manifestation in one particular culture. If we wish to understand the nature of religion, deciding whether it is indeed inevitable in society, these are the types of methodological problems that not only archaeologists have to wrestle with but also anyone who is proposing an evolutionary theory of religion and hence requires it to be evaluated against hard evidence.

The evolution of religion

Having demonstrated that I am at least aware of the methodological problems and pitfalls associated with inferring religious behaviour from archaeological materials, I now complete this short essay with my own particular view about when, why and how the capacity for religious thought evolved. I then consider whether this implies that religion is inevitable in human society.

My starting point is that I am not persuaded that there is any archaeological evidence indicating the presence of religious thought until after the emergence of *Homo sapiens* at *c.* 200,000 years ago.[136] Although it will probably always be impossible to specify what type of religious thought occurred at Blombos Cave other than it falling into Whitehouse's 'imagistic mode', its evidence suggests that some form of religious belief would have existed because, as I explain below, I believe that the cognitive basis of religious thought is the same as for symbolism in general. One may even be able to make the same argument for the considerably older cave site of Pinnacle Point, also on the South African coast but dating to 165,000 years old, in light of evidence for red ochre used for colouring.[137]

Prior to these two sites, I cannot find any persuasive evidence for religious behaviour in the archaeological record, stretching back to

2.5 million years and including that of numerous types of hominins that lived in Africa, Europe and Asia. I am sure that the Neanderthals (*c.* 350,000–30,000 years ago, in Europe and Western Asia) did not bury bodies just to get rid of smelling, decaying corpses; I suspect that they did so because of their deep emotional bonds, their bereavement at loss of family members and friends, and wish to mark the occasion of death.[138] But this need not imply any religious belief.

Similarly, I am not persuaded that any of the so-called symbolic objects from the Neanderthal archaeological record, or that of any hominin other than *Homo sapiens*, are actually objects with symbolic meanings. Some of these were deliberately manufactured, such as the so-called Berekhat Ram 'figurine',[139] but until we find several examples of the same image/object indicating a shared symbolic code, it is academically unsound to interpret these as anything other than utilitarian artefacts.

While non-*Homo sapiens* hominins may have lacked the capacities for religious, artistic or symbolic thought, the cognitive building blocks for these may have been present: they were simply not connected together. In my 1996 book *The Prehistory of the Mind*, I argued that other than *Homo sapiens*, all hominins had a form of domain-specific mentality, and I remain committed to this argument as the most viable interpretation of their archaeological record. In brief, this suggests that large brained hominins such as *Homo heidelbergensis* and *Homo neanderthalensis* had forms of social, technical and natural history intelligence (or cognitive domains, modules or some other term) as fully evolved as that found within *Homo sapiens*. They had, for instance, a capacity for theory of mind – the ability to not only recognize that other individuals had beliefs and desires but to also appreciate that such beliefs and desires were different from their own. This was a key part of their social intelligence, and is likely to have been selected for during the Plio-Pleistocene in the context of ecological pressures to live within large social groups. Similarly, these hominins had the cognitive abilities to mentally rotate artefacts and to understand fracture dynamics of stone and other materials, these being key elements of their technical intelligence and manifest in the sophisticated stone tools they manufactured. Such hominins must have also had profound knowledge and understanding of animal behaviour, of plants, and of natural history in general to have flourished in such a variety of challenging environments during the Pleistocene and throughout the Old World – this most likely being equivalent to the folk biology of recent hunter-gatherers.

While the archaeological evidence is compelling that these hominins had such social, technical and natural history intelligences, it is equally informative that these remained isolated from each other creating a domain-specific mentality quite different to the cognitive fluidity characteristic of modern humans. By cognitive fluidity I mean the capacity – indeed the compulsion – to integrate ways of thinking and bodies of knowledge that had evolved/developed independently to come up with completely novel ideas. This is the essence of the creative mind and was evidently lacking from non-*Homo sapiens* hominins. The archaeological records of *Homo heidelbergensis*, *neanderthalensis* and other hominins may indicate social, technical and natural history intelligences, but they also reflect remarkably monotonous behaviour, almost entirely lacking in any form of inno-vation. For them, the worlds of people, artefacts and animals were relatively isolated from each other and this imposed a major restriction on the nature of thought. For *Homo sapiens* these worlds flow into each other and create ideas about supernatural entities whenever they overlap.

It is indeed from cognitive fluidity that the key features of religious thought emerge. This is from imposing aspects of social intelligence, especially the idea that other human individuals have beliefs, desire and act purposefully, onto non-human animals and inanimate objects. We see this mixing up of categories in the earliest representational art, the cave paintings and carvings from south west France and Spain dating from at least 30,000 years ago. This art includes images of supernatural beings, such as carvings of human bodies with lion heads and paintings that combine elements of several animals and the human form into one imaginary beast. It would be perverse to interpret these as anything other than the Gods and spirits of the Ice Age world; similarly, it becomes compelling to think that the other naturalistic depictions may be of animals that have human-like powers of belief, will and purpose.

The Ice Age art simply provides an example of how the mind of *Homo sapiens* had the characteristic of cognitive fluidity as long ago as 30,000 years. Cognitive fluidity is also responsible, I believe, for the incised ochre objects, shell beads, stone points and red ochre at Blombos Cave at 70,000 years ago and the combination of bodies, architecture and Earth at WF16 at 11,000 years ago. As I have argued elsewhere, cognitive fluidity provides us with the capacity for symbolic, creative and metaphorical thought that underlies both art and science. By enabling the imposition of will and purpose onto inanimate objects, by breaking down the boundaries between the material and immaterial, and between the human, animal and object, cognitive fluidity also provides the capacity for religious thought, most notably the belief in supernatural beings.

Such beings do not have a natural home within the evolved mind – they do not fall into any natural category. This makes them difficult to think about and communicate to others. I, for instance, have never managed to understand what my Christian colleagues mean by 'The Holy Trinity', and I am not persuaded that they share any understanding of this idea between themselves. It is for this reason that religious ideas are so often – perhaps always – anchored outside of the mind by the use of material culture. As such, material culture often becomes an integral part of the religious thought itself.[140] It then becomes far easier to declare what one believes, to reflect on one's own belief, and to communicate that to others – one need do no more than point to an image of the crucifix or an Ice Age lion man carving. So I concur with Matthew Day when he recently wrote in the *Journal of Cognition and Culture* that the broad spectrum of rituals, music, relics, scriptures, statues and buildings typically associated with religious traditions are no longer seen as mere ethnographic icing on the cognitive cake. Rather than cultural 'wrap arounds' that dress up the real cognitive processes going on underneath, they begin to look like central components of the relevant machinery of religious thought.[141]

Is religion inevitable?

Cognitive fluidity was most likely a consequence of the evolution of compositional language that evolved after 200,000 years ago within the *Homo sapiens* lineage.[142] Those individuals who could think in a relatively cognitively fluid manner would have had some reproductive advantage over those who were relatively domain-specific. It allows, for instance, the design of more effective hunting weapons by combining what one knows about artefacts with what one knows about animals – Neanderthals and other non-*Homo sapiens* hominins simply used the same types of hunting weapons for all types of game rather than designing specific artefacts for specific species and circumstances.

Whether the capacity to engage in religious thinking provided a reproductive advantage in itself is less clear. It may have done so, in terms of providing one with a degree of certainty about decisions (because they have been supernaturally ordained) and hence enabling one to act with more confidence (atheists worry too much). All that we can be sure about, however, is that cognitive fluidity provided a propensity to engage in religious thought.

The existence of such a propensity is not sufficient in itself for religion to have become inevitable in human society. But when combined with another propensity of the human mind, to seek power and wealth, this potent mixture does indeed result in the inevitability of religion. Here I am alluding to what used to be referred to as a Marxist view of religion – that this is simply another means by which those with power exploit those without. An individual seeking power and wealth might well achieve these by coercion alone – by either the threat or realization of force. Alternatively, he/she might claim special access to supernatural beings, either offering revelations or proclaiming dire consequences to those who do not act in the manner that he or she (i.e. the supernatural being) desires. Often, these combine so that physical force is legitimized by religious ideology, epitomized in that lovely title of the Holy Roman Empire.

This is a bleak view of the human condition. On the one hand we are predisposed by our evolutionary history to believe in supernatural beings. We can resist such beliefs but this takes a considerable cognitive effort and requires a particular cultural context in which science provides an alternative explanation of natural events. On the other hand, some individuals will take advantage of the existence of this propensity in others as a means to acquire power and wealth for themselves. And so, with the emergence of cognitive fluidity, religion did indeed become inevitable within human society and is likely to always remain so.

10 Artificials, or why Darwin was wrong about humans

Timothy Taylor

With a small axe, I cut off two haunches, leaving the rest of the body to rot where it lay. These creatures were only rude, imperfect machines, with a limited lifespan; they had neither the robustness nor the elegance and perfect functionality of a twin-lens Rolleiflex, I thought, as I looked at their protruding, lifeless eyes.

Michel Houellebecq, "La possibilité d'une île[143]"

Dean's questions

When Wendell Jamieson of the *New York Times* presented a series of questions to experts there was a small catch – they had all been asked by children. I particularly liked 'Mommy, why when you were little was everything black and white?' but the Eastman Kodak guy handled that one. Wendell wanted me to respond to his son, Dean, who, pointing at his little sister Paulina as she disrupted dinnertime with a tantrum, asked in exasperation: 'Why can't we just cook her?' This question became the sub-title of the book *Father Knows Less or: 'Can I Cook My Sister'*.[144]

In my reply to Dean, I explained: 'You cannot just cook and eat your sister, because your father is trying to civilize you . . . Even if you were uncivilized, like the seventy-plus species of mammal who are known cannibals, it would not be your sibling you would kill and eat.' The *kill* was a necessary qualifier. As I explained it to Dean: 'Before farming was developed to provide regular meals, if a member of your family died, it would have made nutritional sense not to waste anything . . . you would not want to attract dangerous meat-eating animals to your camp or allow your enemies a chance of a good feed off your deceased loved one. So in those circumstances, you would have been obliged to eat your sister as part of a solemn, dutiful ritual'.[145] The *solemnity* of ritual is imputed from evidence that archaeologists observe with cut-marked human skeletal remains. In cases of contemporary survival cannibalism too, we rarely 'just' eat other humans, even when culture is stripped away and it becomes 'natural' to do so.

In 1972, Pancho Delgado a trainee lawyer, devout Catholic and rugby player was caught up in an air crash in the high Andes. The Fairchild FH-227 had been carrying a Uruguayan rugby team, manager, trainers, girlfriends, family members – 45 people in all, of whom 13 died on impact. The charter flight was off-course in appalling weather, and search and rescue was called off after a few weeks when it was assumed that, wherever the wreckage lay, no one could possibly still be alive in it. But 70 days later, 16 made it back alive, having survived for many weeks in extreme conditions by eating their dead friends and family – both those who died at first and another 16 who, unwilling to become cannibals, had starved.

Speaking to the potentially scandalized press conference that greeted the miraculous return to Montevideo, Delgado simply said: 'when the moment came when we did not have any more food . . . we thought to ourselves that if Jesus at his last supper had shared his flesh and blood with his apostles, then it was a sign to us that we should do the same – take the flesh and blood as an intimate communion between us all.' Thirty years later, another survivor, Carlos Paez, contradicted this: 'We were hungry, we were cold and we needed to live . . . I don't even think that Delgado himself believed it . . . it was just a very gentle way of saying things, and it was very diplomatic'.[146]

The moral dilemma faced by those who, alive on impact, had to choose whether to try and live in the only possible way, or die to preserve their human dignity, was explicitly addressed by the Vatican in guidance titled *Anthropophagy in extremis.* This argued that, as the souls of the dead were in the care of God, the bodies were desacralized husks and to use them as food was permissible in ultimate need. This not only distanced the cannibals from a charge of irreverence, but also made acceptable the effective suicide of others in their refusal to eat their friends and loved ones, leaving their own mortal salvation in the hands of God (given that they might be rescued at any time, or receive a miracle).[147] In this case, we see that although the survivors dropped through the safety net of culture and became bestial, on their return to civilization they felt the need to add nuance and cultural context to their behaviour, and others helped them to do so. This is something that certainly helps make us human in distinction to animals. We may well doubt, as Charles Darwin did in his *Autobiography*, 'whether humanity is a natural or innate quality.'

This leads to a more general question about human evolution, which Darwin did not have the resources to answer in his time, and which I believe he got wrong. Or, at least, if he did not, Darwinists have. Since my explanation about why he should not eat his sister, Wendell has fielded another of Dean's questions to me, 'If I lived in nature, would I survive?' The implication, that the family apartment in which Dean lives in New York is not natural, is at the heart of the matter.

I replied that there were laws of physics and laws of biology that conditioned survival in nature – essentially the limits of physical tolerances and the body's own adaptive mechanisms – but that, critically, Dean had a cultural inheritance that changed the rules: 'extra stuff, like mobile phones, taxis and hospitals.' I pointed out to Dean that, far from technology being modern, it has modified our physics and biology throughout our evolution. Our biological evolution was actually technologically enabled. The first stone tools are over 2.5 million years old, dating to before we had really evolved as humans. It looks as if only after we got levers, knives and axes did we lose our sharp teeth, big muscles and claws. So my hunch is that the tools – the artificial things we are so used to – actually allowed us to evolve. 'Dean, you are not a natural object yourself,' I concluded.

The idea of a third realm of powers and laws is growing out of artificial intelligence theory. Ray Kurzweil has called this realm the 'Technium', and looked forward to a point which he calls 'the singularity', when computers become more intelligent than humans. Although some of this vision makes sense to me, it also presupposes some sharp biology–technology divide. This, in my view, does not exist. The evolution of humans is actually the history of elision and synergy between a biological substrate and an artificial realm.

'Intelligent' design? The fitness paradox

The term *artificials* is a homage to the John Tradescants, both father and son, 17th-century royal gardeners and the founder collectors of what became the Ashmolean Museum. In the catalogue to their 'Cabinet of Curiosities' – filled with 'all kinds of shells, the hand of a mermaid, the hand of a mummy, a very natural wax hand under glass, all kinds of precious stones, coins, a picture wrought in feathers, a small piece of wood from the cross of Christ', as Georg Christoph Stirn described it[148] in 1638 – they made a principal distinction between 'Naturalls' – those things for which nature alone was responsible – and 'Artificialls'– those artefacts that involved the recombination/modification of natural material to make objects of material culture. Thus began the history of comparison between the natural and the artificial, in which principles from the latter have often been imputed to the former.

Although 'Intelligent Design' is a recent tag, the thinking goes back at least as far as William Paley, whose *Natural Theology* so inspired Darwin. Paley's most famous analogy was how we logically infer from finding a watch that a watchmaker exists. Presented with mechanisms in the natural world which were so much more complicated than watches ('in a degree which exceeds all computation'), Paley's God was the divine and supreme watchmaker. Paley was overwhelmingly enthusiastic about the Great Designer's works: 'The spine, or backbone, is a chain of joints of very wonderful construction. Various, difficult and almost inconsistent offices were to be executed by the same instrument. It was to be firm, yet flexible . . . firm, to support the erect position of the body; flexible, to allow of the bending of the trunk in all degrees of curvature.' The stabilizing condyles of a hare's neatly slotted vertebrae were 'the very contrivance which is employed in the famous iron-bridge at my door at Bishop-Wearmouth.'[149]

But Darwin was to uncover a law-like system of natural selection that allowed the Great Designer to be dispensed with, and replaced with an essentially directionless, or at least director-less, evolution. His scientific method, like that of Alexander von Humboldt before him, combined accumulated observations (data) within a daring imaginative framework (theory). The result was a principle of evolution of forms through time, in which natural selection acted on each generation as it descended with modification from its immediate ancestors. Although Darwin wrote that 'our ignorance of the laws of variation is profound,' he nevertheless guessed rightly that a recombination involved in sexual reproduction mixed up what he thought of as the 'germ plasm,' the formal blueprint for the next generation. The scrambling was limited by viability, and resulted in offspring that typically differed from one another and from their parents in minor features. The effects of chance and the rigours of the environment, operating over extremely long time periods, were the ultimate causes of speciation and extinction.

Darwin lacked access to the mechanism of recombination, and could only partly explain the gradual emergence of ever more complex forms through diversification. Others have covered this ground thoroughly, including Richard Dawkins in his aptly named *The Blind Watchmaker.*[150] But what neither Paley, Darwin nor Dawkins appreciated is the suspicious difference between, say, a hare's spine, with its neatly interlocking, stabilized vertebrae, and a human spine in all its unreliable, painful glory. Darwin was correct to note the similarity between the gorilla spine and the human one, but what he should have seen is that the human spine *is*, more or less, a gorilla one, unconvincingly adapted for a fully bipedal gait. The reality is that humans, in particular, are very poorly 'designed', whether by the perfect Creator or the fiery forge of Darwinian redaction.

Human beings should not exist. Our skulls are so large that we risk being stuck and dying even as we are struggling to be born. Helped out by a technical team – obstetrician, midwife and a battery of bleeping machines – the unwieldy cranium is followed into the light by a pathetic excuse for a mammalian body. And there we are screaming, hairless and so muscularly feeble that we have no chance of supporting our heads properly for months after birth. These initial inadequacies are just the start of a litany of one utterly mad design decision after another – inefficient digestion, bad insulation, tender feet, fragile nails, feeble teeth, poor sense of smell and weak vision. How does a species in which unaided birth is frequently near fatal and in which progeny need several years of adult support before they can dress themselves, not just evolve but become the *dominant* species on its planet? Why, as a minimum, couldn't human children have been born with some nice fur, rather than requiring their human parents to devise ways of killing and skinning dangerous animals to get *their* fur off them and make it into clothing? How is that an *advantage*?

There are many instances in evolution where an attribute carries a history, something vestigial, something that can make do for a creature, despite its evolutionary origins in an earlier, different environment. Consider human eyes. The existence of eyes is one of the favourite battle grounds of creationists and Intelligent Design adherents as they attempt to rubbish Darwinian evolution. In stark contrast to my opening quotation from the French novelist Michel Houellebecq, the anti-evolution site *Collapse of Evolution* (www.allaahuakba.net) informs us that 'Cameras are one of the greatest products of the technology of the 20th century. The eyes of humans and other living beings, however, are much more complex and perfect than the most advanced camera in the world. The superior design in the eye can never be explained by chance and it constitutes concrete evidence for creation.' Yet *International Market News* reports[151] that 'the key driver in the size and performance of the optical goods market is, of course, the number of people wearing glasses and contact lenses. These consumers make up 65 per cent of the UK population.'

Although 'natural' selection was at the core of Darwin's system, 'artificial' selection was his key metaphor for inter-generational change and the concept of fitness. As a member of various British pigeon fancying and racing societies, he was aware of at least six very distinct bird-types descendant from breeding experiments with rock doves (*Columba livia*) in Belgium from the 1820s onwards. Before this were several millennia of domestication, as such birds were widely used in the Ancient and Classical worlds to carry news of victory home, as they did from the first Olympic Games in 776 BC, and to Rome when Caesar conquered Gaul.

Pigeons are no longer wholly natural, having been tweaked biologically by cultural pressures. But the category artificials stretches even beyond domestic animals. The human eye, for example, with all its modern corrective needs, has experienced a peculiar 'negative' reverberation of cultural pressures. Long ago, Jean-Paul Sartre used the term 'practico-inert'[152] for the way in which technological living has unintended consequences. Each solution requires greater technological elaboration, which creates further knock-ons, needs and problems requiring technological fixes in a potentially endless chain of entailment. A brief account might go like this: the ancient development of lens technology, probably primarily by jewellers, allowed congenitally poor sight to be corrected at least by Roman times. Over the centuries, as the technology became cheaper and better understood, nearly everyone could have glasses and even the radically short-sighted were able to discern mates of the opposite sex across a smoky ballroom and reproduce. The result is that, for many human communities in the modern world, the selection pressure on naturally acute vision has largely been removed. It is quite possible that future optics, by visualizing a lethal strain of influenza virus, or discerning an Earth-bound asteroid in time for it to be diverted from fatal collision, might increase our species' inclusive fitness in a decisive way. Material culture, in allowing human adaptation to many specific environments, has also allowed us to perceive 'environments' at other levels, microcosmic and cosmic, and avert threats that other, purely biological, species would not be able to recognize.

This is not the whole story either of optics or of the range of variance of human eyes, but it serves to show how cultural interventions increasingly become part of success, beyond mere biological 'survival of the fittest'. It goes way beyond the standard recognition that human culture helps us adapt to natural environments, or that humans modify their environments to suit themselves (as hermit crabs do when building their own shells). The realm of artificials has brought into being a new set of unfolding rules.

Neither necessary nor sufficient

My answer to Dean indicated three fundamental systems: the inanimate, the animate and material culture. Each is populated by entities of different type, and display distinctive and specific patterning (see Figure 3). These categories help clarify the problem with recent arguments suggesting that human material cultures, in addition to animate humans themselves, conform to Darwinian laws. Most well known is Dawkins' assertion that culture spreads via replicative units, known as memes, whose relative success or failure is generated by the same kind of selection pressures that act on biological entities. The essential point is that gene-based life evolves in a more complex way than inanimate chemical elements and cultural objects – artefacts and technology (see Figure 3) – evolve in a yet more complex way, and represent a further

Figure 3 An unmodified pebble (geological), a fragment of fossil ammonite (biological) and a section of flint blade (cultural).

step change, partly because they involve many interacting components that cannot easily be pinned down.

A useful example to consider here might be the definition of the meme for 'car', in the way that we might define a gene for, say, insulin production. Consider a car with four wheels. Four wheels is typical but not necessary: some cars have three. Four wheels is also not sufficient to define the category 'car', as carts and vans may have four wheels too. The emphasis on 'sufficient' and 'necessary' is deliberate. Generally, biological entities can be classified according to attributes that are at once sufficient and necessary for group inclusion. A car, however, belongs to what an archaeologist would call a polythetic set: 'a group of entities such that each entity possesses a large number of the attributes of the group, each attribute is shared by large numbers of entities and no single attribute is both sufficient and necessary for group membership'.[153]

Many of the car's necessary things, like seats, will be necessities both in other vehicles and in non-vehicles, and no one thing will have the power that, say, a specific biological genome has in defining its 'species' or kind. Cars do not exist either like individual species of mammal, or at some other taxonomic level, such as the taxon 'mammal', or 'vertebrate.' The same is true for stone axes, chairs, plates, spectacles, telescopes, microscopes, space-ships, hospitals, computers . . . a truth that, it turns out, is sufficient in itself to be fatal for the 'meme' concept, not to mention the other objections to memes raised by philosophers, social anthropologists and cultural historians.[154] The concept is incoherent and cannot do more than faintly approximate how cultural traits are actually transmitted.

Crudely put, material objects are not definable as species, do not mate with one another to produce variation, and have a fitness for purpose that is judged within complex and idiosyncratic cultural milieux. Whether there are any 'laws' of cultural transmission is an open question. Certainly there are many mechanisms, often of a complex kind that challenge analysis and interpretation. A developing body of theory called 'materiality theory' examines how objects enable actions, how intelligence extends into the world of 'things', and how that world, in full circle, structures own our culture.[155] The artificial realm operates in a more complex way than biological systems. Its variation cannot be accounted for by Darwinian mechanisms alone, just as biological systems cannot, in turn, be described by reference to physical dynamics alone.

I now want to suggest that the artificial realm was not brought into existence by humans, but that artefacts brought humans into existence. The first chipped stone tool precedes significant hominin brain expansion by 0.5 million years. The extra edge that stone tools provided, followed by the first use of fire to cook and soften food, allowed hominin teeth (especially canines) to become smaller and chewing muscles to diminish. This change then freed our ancestors' evolution from these physical restrictions to the cranial vault, potentially allowing larger brains and greater intelligence to evolve. A further, oft-overlooked but critical, restriction on brain size remained in the shape of the tortuously narrow pelvis that allowed the emergence of bipedalism in small-brained australopithecines. This barrier was also most likely removed by material culture operating in advance of major cognitive development, in this case through baby-carrying technologies. The sling would have allowed infants to be born more undeveloped and subsequently free to complete what was previously intra-uterine brain growth outside, within an increasingly culture-soaked context, and so on.

Our evolution has been led, I think, by material culture and its unplanned consequences. These progressively alter the geometry of the possible. With each technological addition, from stone tools through to laser eye surgery, there is a reverberation from the artificial onto the biological. Biological fitness, in natural selection terms, becomes less and less the issue, and new and highly diverse worlds of human activity and existence are brought into being. Humans themselves, as anthropologist Clifford Geertz said,[156] are cultural artefacts.

Materiality and God

I have argued for three realms of entities: inanimate physics and chemistry, animate biology, and the complex realm of artificials. As simple mechanical replicators, viruses are on the cusp of what we might call an 'entity phase transition', being somewhere between inanimate and animate systems. In like manner, humans appear to inhabit another entity phase transition, half way between biological and material cultural systems.

I hope that telling Dean that he is not a natural object will make sense to him, and would perhaps also have made some sense to Darwin. Darwin deplored the wretchedness of the Fuegans, living naked in Patagonia, as being a result of their relative lack of material culture, without drawing the conclusion that humans minus a certain threshold level of artificial aid are wretched indeed.

One aspect of our non-naturalness is the cultural evolution of ideas of gods or 'God'. It is worth going back about 30,000 years to the rapid development of figurative art in the Gravettian or Middle Upper Palaeolithic period of Europe. In creating miniature human and animal bodies in materials such as antler, ivory and limestone, Ice Age hunters were able to enculturate nature. At the same time as communities were growing and searching for new mechanisms of social control, religion, ritual, sympathetic magic, and sacred art set up a mental resonance. If painters and carvers could bring vivid images into the cultural order, then some corresponding power may have been felt, behind the scenes, creating the living order. This sort of thinking underpins the religion of many creator gods even today, and is present in the obsession of the anti-Darwinists with seeing the biological world as somehow designed.

Darwin's own mature religious reservations may have been conditioned not so much by his crisis of faith following the harrowing death of a beloved daughter, but that his system denied God a hands-on designer role, undermining a familiar and comfortable mode of thought. It left no space for visualizing a replacement except in highly abstract philosophical ways. That Darwin appreciated that such ways were fully possible may explain his devout agnosticism better than considering it a euphemistic atheism borne of mere politeness to his clerical friends and acquaintances.

By using material culture to modify what was around us, we have been able to so far outstrip other biological entities that we have actually started to consciously engineer them. In any case, my argument is far more damaging to Intelligent Design than to the kinds of thinking Darwin typically approved. Yet Darwin himself might have agreed with my argument, had he known what we do now about human anatomic deficits, and the archaeology of the long-term interplay of material cultural evolution and human biological evolution, with its curious leads and lags. No wonder we are obsessed with ideas of fitness for purpose and hidden designers. Perfecting things to accomplish tasks is what we do par excellence.

Part III Is religion harmful? From brains to societies

11 Brain science and belief

Andrew Newberg

When considering the relationship between science and religion in modern society, it seems critical to establish where within the human person the foundations of all of our notions about the world originate. After all, science and religion are both systems of thought that enable us to deal with and understand the world. They are obviously based upon different fundamental principles. However, the central issue is to explore how we as human beings come to any understanding about our world. As a neuroscientist, it appears to me that the brain is that part of ourselves that ultimately interprets various inputs and ideas into a clear and coherent world view. But there is a fundamental paradox, which is that we can never escape our brain to determine if what we think and understand, on the inside, is related at all to what is on the outside. Of course, for our survival, it is important that there be a good correspondence, but from the brain's perspective, adaptability is probably far more relevant than accuracy. This problem is what has led me to explore the nature and origin of human beliefs. In fact, I would argue that because of the paradox of being trapped in our brain, everything we feel, think and do with respect to the world is necessarily a belief – something that we take to be true even though we can't fully know if it is. Here I want to explore where beliefs come from, and to see how they relate to science, religion and all other aspects of the human world.

The power of beliefs

The importance of beliefs is best exemplified by how individuals responded to our study, at the University of Pennsylvania, of changes in the brain's activity during various religious and spiritual experiences.[157] For example, after we performed brain scans on Franciscan nuns, the nuns felt that the various changes we observed in their brain supported their initial religious beliefs. They were very pleased that the results demonstrated significant changes in the brain when they were deeply engaged in prayer. They felt this showed that God interacted not only with their spirit, but their entire being, including their brain and body. The changes in the brain during prayer thus supported their original beliefs that God had an important part in their lives. On the other hand, several individuals who described themselves as atheists felt that the brain scans were completely supportive of their notion that there was no God, and that religion and spirituality were merely manifestations of the human brain. Thus, for them, the brain scans supported their beliefs that religion and God were nothing more than a product of the human brain rather than the brain being a product of some infinite, all powerful God.

These discordant interpretations of the data were extremely intriguing to me and suggested the importance of an individual's initial beliefs in interpreting any particular body of data. Unfortunately, very little has actually been done to evaluate the effects of beliefs and their origins. This is surprising, as beliefs are ultimately one of the most important functions of the human brain (see Lewis Wolpert's Chapter 8). In fact, I would argue that the human brain is essentially a believing machine, and that it has no other choice but to create beliefs about every aspect of our lives – religious, spiritual, political and moral.

There are many examples of the incredible power of belief in our lives. We see this strongly in the context of the placebo effect in which the human brain is capable of creating changes in various aspects of our overall health and well-being. Recent functional brain imaging studies have shown that the placebo is an extremely specific and complex process in the brain. For example, brain images from individuals with depression have shown that a placebo can alter the serotonin system of the brain, the same brain areas affected by drugs such as Prozac and Zoloft. Studies of individuals with Parkinson's disease have shown that those responding to a placebo have increases in the release of dopamine, even though this is a neurodegenerative disease that causes severe decreases in dopamine function. And finally, placebos have even been shown to relieve pain by triggering the release of endorphins, the opiate system in the brain.

Of course, the power of beliefs is highly evident in religious and political systems. We see beliefs in various aspects of humanity, such as freedom, equality and liberty as contributing to some of the great societies in the world. Conversely, beliefs regarding racial superiority, opposing religions or opposing political systems can lead to wide-spread conflicts and hatred. Given the power of beliefs, let us take a closer look at what beliefs are and how they arise in the brain.

What is a belief?

The *Oxford English Dictionary* defines a belief as 'a feeling that something exists or is true especially one without proof.' This is a particularly interesting use of the word 'proof'. After all, what constitutes a proof is heavily dependent on an individual's perspective. For a philosopher, a proof may be a particularly complex line of rational argument. For a medical scientist, it may be a randomized, double-blind controlled trial. With religious and spiritual beliefs, however, there is a great deal of contention regarding what constitutes evidence and proof. Many atheists ask why the religious individual believes in God, when there is 'no evidence' that God actually exists. On the other hand, most religious individuals feel that they have ample 'evidence' that God exists in their lives, citing births of children, marriages or some unusual set of experiences. Clearly, what evidence constitutes a proof is completely dependent on one's pre-existing beliefs. An atheist and a religious person hold different beliefs about the nature of the Universe and what constitutes a proof, yet each set of beliefs can be flawed.

As a cognitive neuroscientist, I prefer the following definition:

> A belief is defined biologically and psychologically as any perception, cognition, or emotion that the brain assumes, consciously or unconsciously, to be true.

This definition accounts for the multiple aspects in the origins of beliefs. Beliefs arise from our sensory perceptions of the world, our interactions with others, the ways in which we process information cognitively, and how we use our emotional brain to make certain decisions. Beliefs may be both conscious or unconscious, and psychology has long dealt with the impact of the unconscious mind on human behaviours and thoughts. We often respond to other individuals (or stimuli) via unconsciously assumed beliefs.

Underlying the question of origin of our beliefs is, why do we believe in anything at all? The human brain exists within a virtually limitless Universe. Out of all of the potential information available to the brain, it ultimately must restrict its processing to a very small amount. While reading this chapter, you are aware primarily of the various stimuli in your immediate surroundings and from the book you are holding. You are not aware of happenings in another city, another country or elsewhere in the Universe. The brain not only restricts its input of information, but it transfers an even smaller percentage up to your consciousness. Only the information that arises in your consciousness helps you form your primary beliefs about the world. In fact, from this entire book, you are likely only to retain several salient points in your consciousness that may ultimately affect your beliefs in life.

Since the brain filters out so much information, it has no choice but to construct beliefs about the world, to help us navigate and behave properly. As many philosophers have argued, it is impossible for us to know whether or not our perceptions and beliefs correspond to what is actually out there in the world. The only way to actually determine this would be to somehow escape one's brain, to judge objectively from the outside. Hence science, as practised by us, may never enable us to determine how accurately the brain perceives and understands the world. In fact, many scientific studies demonstrate just the opposite. The brain is notoriously limited in its ability to accurately perceive the world, and it never reveals to us consciously when it has injected inaccuracy into our thinking. The brain constantly makes us feel as if we have a complete and thorough view of the entire world. But the evidence clearly suggests otherwise.

The origin of beliefs

If beliefs are formed from our perceptions, cognitions, emotions and social interactions, we can explore each of these processes individually, to determine precisely what and how flaws may be introduced. As visual, auditory or tactile information arrives, the brain often has problems assimilating such information. Optical illusions, magicians, things that we think we hear or unusual perceptions of the body, all should make us pause whenever we think that we actually perceive something correctly. Often, 'seeing is believing', although what we see is not always accurately reflected in the human brain, eliciting a variety of different beliefs.

Cognitive processing functions of the human brain are not only for evaluating information arriving through our senses, but also for acquiring and maintaining our beliefs. Our cognitive processes will evaluate a new idea to determine if it 'makes sense' in the context of our existing belief systems. Once a belief is incorporated, we will then use our cognitive abilities to support and defend that belief. Thus, when our beliefs are contested, we typically offer a defence that we see as logical and rational, which is why our detractors often seem irrational or illogical. In a disagreement, both view the other as irrational because their brains actually are functioning similarly.

I place the cognitive functions of the brain that affect our beliefs into the following categories: *causal, binary, quantitative, existential, holistic, reductionistic* and *abstract.*[158] The causal, binary and existential functions are particularly important to religion and spirituality.

The *causal function* allows us to identify causes and effects, and to predict future events based on current information. This is essentially what underlies the science of causal relationships among physical entities such as atoms, molecules or stars. Then if one applies the causal function to the human realm, the result is social science and psychology, which is more problematic, but we can still advance understanding of behaviour and thought by using prior information. Finally, when one applies the causal function to the Universe as a whole, the result tends towards ultimate causes of the Universe. As

David Wilkinson discusses, this leads to ideas about God or ultimate reality that depend on the individual's perspective.

Cognitive processes limit our ability to accurately understand the world and do not have any direct bearing on what the world actually is. A person whose brain could not understand cause and effect might understand God as the ultimate love of the Universe, but such a person could never understand God as the *cause* of things in the Universe. In any case, this has no bearing on whether or not God actually *is* a fundamental cause of the Universe.

The *binary function* enables us to set up opposites, such as good versus bad or right versus wrong (the famous French anthropologist, Claude Levi-Strauss, made a similar identification in his classic, *The Raw and the Cooked*). In monotheistic religions, a fundamental opposition is the relationship between God and human beings. After all, how are we as finite, mortal beings, to have any kind of understanding or connection with something that is supposedly infinite, eternal and all-powerful? In fact, it is through the processes of religious ritual that the opposite of God and human beings is ultimately resolved so that we do have an understanding of how to have that interaction. This usually occurs through the induction of the holistic functions of the brain through the rhythmic process of ritual.

The *existential function* of the brain is crucial to how we experience and identify reality, by assigning sensory information to things that exist or do not exist in the world. You recognize the objects of a dream, for instance, as distinct from everyday reality. This is part of how individuals come to the notion that the material world is all that there is, with no supernatural level. However, for those who have had profound spiritual or mystical experiences, one of the most common descriptions we hear is that it feels 'more real' then our everyday reality experiences. This creates quite a conundrum from the scientific and philosophical perspective, which function within our everyday reality. When a mystical experience is perceived to be more real than everyday reality (also see Lewis Wolpert's Chapter 8), rationality and science are similarly perceived as inferior to this higher sense. Profound mystical experiences lie at the heart of most religious traditions, and whether they truly represent a higher level of reality remains an open question. In Judeo-Christian traditions, figures such as Moses or St. Teresa of Avila had deeply real experiences of communicating with God. Religion is replete with such experiences and derives much of its meaning from them.

Affected by external stimuli as well as previously held internal beliefs, our cognitive processes are easily manipulated. For example, Republicans and Democrats look at the same data about the environment or the economy and come to completely different conclusions; the rational functions of their brains work similarly, but are quite affected by the particular ideological starting position. This is also why the nuns and the atheists interpreted our brain scan data in completely different ways. One study clearly demonstrated that people of all different beliefs – from atheist to religious – make logical mistakes when confronted with ideas contrary to their prevailing belief system.

Emotions, like rational cognitive functions, help us identify and maintain our beliefs. A new idea that 'feels good' to us is much more likely to be incorporated into our existing belief system. On the other hand, an idea that seems discordant with our beliefs often makes us feel anxious and upset, and we are far less likely to accept it. We often defend our beliefs vigorously, using our emotions, as our beliefs are crucial for our overall survival and well-being, determining how to live, behave and interact with others.

When faced with an individual who disagrees with our belief system, we typically have one of two choices. The first is to think that our own belief system may be incorrect – a notoriously problematic position for the brain to be in. The second is to assume the other individual is incorrect, which is much easier emotionally, since we can continue to feel good about our own belief system while recognizing the problems of another. These emotions, however, can turn to hatred and antagonism, especially if an individual still disagrees after we have explained our rational support for our own belief system. We might identify the other as a bad or evil person, or even someone who exists outside of our normal sense of reality. In such a case, we would have no problem engendering ill will, antagonism or violence towards the other person, if it further supports our own beliefs and eliminates the inappropriate and inaccurate alternative.

We often like to feel as if we have come to our own good sense on our own accord, but the data support a far different view. We are heavily influenced by other individuals around us. Our beliefs are rarely our own. Our beliefs begin through the interaction with our parents in early life. They instil in us beliefs about how the world works, and about morals, politics and religion. In fact, most studies have shown that individuals continue to maintain the political and religious belief systems that their parents had. Such beliefs can be changed over time, but this typically depends on other individuals that we meet throughout our lives including teachers, peers and colleagues. It is also important to note that we are heavily influenced by all of these individuals and that our beliefs frequently will conform to those around us. This is a much easier situation for the brain, since it is not comfortable with a substantial antagonism or disagreement. We would be in difficulty if all those around us disagreed, which is partly why we seek out like-minded individuals. It would be very difficult for a Republican to live in a completely Democratic community, or to be the only Christian among a group of Muslims. We are far more likely to congregate with individuals who look at, and believe in, the world similarly, since this lowers our levels of stress and anxiety and makes us feel much more supported and comfortable with the belief systems that we have.

The neurobiology of beliefs

Given that the perceptual, cognitive, emotional and social processes influence on our beliefs, we can now look more deeply at the neurobiology of where beliefs come from. Ultimately, our beliefs are ingrained deeply within the neural connections of the brain, and the more we focus on a particular belief, the more that belief becomes our reality. This is based on the premise that 'neurons that fire together are wired together'. Within the brain, special support nerve cells and molecules help neurons to strengthen their connections the more they fire together. This is why when you are growing up and trying to learn that 1 + 2 = 3, you repeat this phrase several times until the neural connection sticks. At that point it becomes a belief that you hold onto for the rest of your life. This also explains why practices like meditation, prayer and ritual are so valuable to religions because they continuously repeat the specific ideological foundations of the religious system. By meditating on God, praying to God, reading about God, celebrating holidays about the past interactions with God, the individuals begins to see God as their reality. In fact, their brain cannot do otherwise. As I mentioned previously, this has no bearing on what reality actually is. Our beliefs may or may not accurately reflect reality, and they can be easily manipulated through various perceptual, cognitive and social processes.

Since there is a fundamental dichotomy between the perceptions of our brains versus the real world, *everything* that we think and understand about the world is necessarily a belief. We have no other option but to create beliefs to guide how to behave and interact with the world: beliefs about our jobs, our relationships and the Universe itself. We are forever trapped within our own belief systems, and can never know exactly if we are correct. Atheists or fundamentalists, their brains are in the same boat; neither has any true way of knowing what is real or accurate, as their brains create for them their experience of reality.

This has been part of the reason for my great interest in the study of mystical experiences. Such experiences are often perceived to be even 'more real' than our everyday experience of reality. Furthermore, these are one of the few types of experiences in which people actually describe that they get beyond, or transcend, their own selves. These experiences may offer hope to somehow find out what is truly out there, by actually getting outside of our brains. At the moment, there is no way of knowing whether or not these individuals truly do get beyond their own brain, but given the nature of the experience and the incredibly compelling sense of the realness that it carries, I think it is worth taking a very serious look at these experiences.

Our brain scans have demonstrated substantial activity in the brain when engaged in expert meditation and prayer, particularly in the parts that help us to focus attention. This suggests the brain is highly engaged, and recent evidence suggests that the brain itself is changed by such practices over time, which could help us understand how beliefs themselves are altered and affected. Such studies might also help us understand why the focus of attention on a particular belief such as God creates such a powerful experience for the individual and establishes a God-based belief system as a critical component of that person's brain.

Credo ergo sum

I finish with several conclusions. The first is that the brain is a believing machine for all of us. We all need to create beliefs about every aspect of our life. However, the brain has many potential flaws that lead to beliefs which may or may not be accurately reflecting what is out there in reality. Second, for us to be 'better believers' we must continuously challenge our beliefs that arise from perceptual, cognitive, emotional and social influences. Third, we all should be a bit more compassionate about those who come to beliefs that are different from our own. We need to recognize our emotional responses to those who disagree with us and realize that all of our brains are trying to do the best that they can at interpreting an extensive amount of information about an essentially infinite world. Finally, if the brain truly is a believing machine, we must acknowledge that beliefs affect every part of our lives, and every part of our lives affects our beliefs. The edge of our reason as human beings is defined ultimately by the beliefs that our brain creates. One might even go as far as a paraphrasing of Descartes' '*cogito ergo sum*' (I think therefore I am) to '*credo ergo sum*' – I believe therefore I am.

12 Why Richard Dawkins is wrong about religion

David Sloan Wilson[159]

Richard Dawkins and I share much in common. We are both biologists by training who have written widely about evolutionary theory. We share an interest in culture as an evolutionary process in its own right. We are both atheists in our personal convictions, who have written books on religion. In *Darwin's Cathedral*[160] I attempted to contribute to the relatively new field of evolutionary religious studies. When Dawkins' *The God Delusion*[161] was published I naturally assumed that he was basing his critique of religion on the scientific study of religion from an evolutionary perspective. I regret to report otherwise. He has not done any original work on the subject, he has not fairly represented the work of his colleagues. Hence this critique of *The God Delusion*, the larger issues at stake.

Where we agree and where we part company

In *The God Delusion,* Dawkins makes it clear that he loathes religion for its intolerance, blind faith, cruelty, extremism, abuse and prejudice. He attributes these problems to religion and thinks that the world would be a better place without it. Given recent events in the Middle East and even here in America, it is understandable why he might draw such a conclusion, but the question is: What's evolution got to do with it?

Dawkins and I agree that evolutionary theory provides a powerful framework for studying religion, and we even agree on some of the details, so it is important to pinpoint exactly where we part company. Evolutionists employ a number of hypotheses to study any trait, even something as mundane as the spots on a guppy. Is it an adaptation that evolved by natural selection? If so, did it evolve by benefiting whole groups, compared to other groups, or individuals compared to other individuals within groups? With cultural evolution there is a third possibility. Since cultural traits pass from person to person, they bear an intriguing resemblance to disease organisms. Perhaps they evolve to enhance their own transmission without benefiting human individuals or groups.

If the trait is not an adaptation, then it can nevertheless persist in the population for a variety of reasons. Perhaps it was adaptive in the past but not the present, such as our eating habits, which make sense in the food-scarce environment of our ancestors but not with a McDonald's on every corner. Perhaps the trait is a by-product of another adaptation. For example, moths use celestial light sources to orient their flight (an adaptation), but this causes them to spiral towards earthly light sources such as a streetlamp or a flame (a costly by-product), as Dawkins so beautifully recounts in *The God Delusion.* Finally, the trait might be selectively neutral and persist in the population by genetic or cultural drift.

Dawkins and I agree that these major hypotheses provide an excellent framework for organizing the study of religion, which by itself is an important achievement. We also agree that the hypotheses are not mutually exclusive. Evolution is a messy, complicated process, like the creation of laws and sausages, and all of the major hypotheses might be relevant to some degree. Nevertheless, real progress requires determining which hypotheses are most important for the evolution of particular traits. The spots on a guppy might seem parochial, but they are famous among biologists as a case study of evolutionary analysis. They can be explained primarily as adaptations in response to two powerful selective forces: predators remove the most conspicuous males from the population, whereas female guppies mate with the most conspicuous males. The interaction between these two selection pressures explains an impressive amount of detail about guppy spots — why males have them and females don't, why males are more colourful in habitats without predators, and even why the spots are primarily red when the predators are crustaceans (whose visual system is blind to the colour red), as opposed to fish (whose visual system is sensitive to the colour red). Guppy spots could have been selectively neutral or a by-product of some other trait, but that's not the way the facts fell.

Richard Dawkins and Stephen Jay Gould: Strange bedfellows

The late Harvard evolutionary biologist Stephen Jay Gould famously criticized his colleagues for seeing adaptations where they don't exist. His metaphor for a by-product was the spandrel, the triangular space that inevitably results when arches are placed next to each other. Arches have a function but spandrels do not, even though they can acquire a secondary function, such as providing a decorative space. Gould accused his colleagues of inventing 'just-so stories' about traits as adaptations, without good proof, and being blind to the possibility of by-products and other non-adaptive outcomes of evolution.

Gould had a point, but he failed to give equal time to the opposite problem of failing to see adaptations where they do exist. Suppose that you are a biologist who becomes interested in explaining the bump on the nose of a certain species of shark. Perhaps it is just a by-product of the way that shark noses develop, as Gould speculated for the human chin. Perhaps it is a callous that forms when the sharks root around in the sand. If so, then it would be an adaptation but not a very complicated one. Perhaps it is a wart, formed by a virus. If so, then it might be an adaptation for the virus but not the shark. Or perhaps it is an organ for detecting the weak electrical signals of prey hidden in the sand. If so, then it would be a complex adaptation.

Few experiences are more thrilling for a biologist than to discover a complex adaptation. Myriad details that previously defied explanation become interpretable as an interlocking system with a purpose. Non-adaptive traits can also be complex, but the functional nature of a complex adaptation guides its analysis from beginning to end. Failing to recognize complex adaptations when they exist is as big a mistake as seeing them where they don't exist. Only hard empirical work – something equivalent to the hundreds of person-years spent studying guppy spots from an evolutionary perspective – can settle the issue.

Dawkins argued on behalf of adaptationism in his debates with Gould and would probably agree with everything I have said so far. For religion, however, he argues primarily on behalf of non-adaptation. As he sees it, people are attracted to religion the way that moths are attracted to flames. Perhaps religious impulses were adapted to the tiny social groups of our ancestral past, but not the mega-societies of the present. If current religious beliefs are adaptive at all, it is only for the beliefs themselves as cultural parasites on their human hosts, like the demons of old that were thought to possess people. That is why Dawkins calls God a delusion. The least likely possibility for Dawkins is the group-level adaptation hypothesis. Religions are emphatically not elaborate systems of beliefs and practices that define, motivate, coordinate and police groups of people for their own good.

For the good of the group?

To understand Dawkins' scepticism about the group-level benefits of religion, it is necessary to trace the history of 'for the good of the group' thinking in evolutionary theory. Groups can be adaptive only if their members perform services for each other, yet these services are often vulnerable to exploitation by more self-serving individuals within the same group. Fortunately, groups of individuals who practice mutual aid can out-compete groups whose members do not.

According to this reasoning, traits that are 'for the good of the group' require a process of between-group selection to evolve and tend to be undermined by selection within groups. Darwin was the first person to reason this way about the evolution of human morality and self-sacrificial traits in other animals. Unfortunately, his insight was not shared by many biologists during the first half of the 20th century, who uncritically assumed that adaptations evolve at all levels of the biological hierarchy – for the good of the individual, group, species or ecosystem – without requiring a corresponding process of natural selection at each level. When the need for group selection was acknowledged, it was often assumed that between-group selection easily prevailed against within-group selection. This can be called The Age of Naïve Groupism, and it ended during the 1960s and 1970s, thanks largely to two books: George C. Williams' 1966 *Adaptation and Natural Selection*[162] and Richard Dawkins' 1976 *The Selfish Gene*.[163]

In *Adaptation and Natural Selection*, Williams affirmed the logic of multi-level selection but then added an empirical claim: Even though between-group selection is theoretically possible, in the real world it is invariably trumped by within-group selection. Virtually all adaptations evolve at the individual level and even examples of apparent altruism must be explained in terms of self-interest. It was this empirical claim that ended The Age of Naïve Groupism and initiated what can be called The Age of Individualism, which lasted for the rest of the 20th century and in some respects is still with us.

Another theme developed by Williams was the concept of the gene as the fundamental unit of selection. In sexually reproducing species, an individual is a unique collection of genes that will never occur again. Individuals therefore lack the permanence to be acted upon by natural selection over multiple generations. According to Williams, genes are the fundamental unit of natural selection because they have the permanence that individuals (much less groups) lack.

In many respects, and by his own account, Williams was interpreting ideas for a broader audience that began with Darwin and were refined by theoretical biologists such as Sewall Wright, Ronald Fisher and J.B.S. Haldane. The concept of the gene as the fundamental unit of selection, for example, is identical to the concept of average effects in population genetics theory, which averages the fitness of alternative genes across all of the individual genotypes and environmental contexts experienced by the genes. A decade later, Dawkins played the role of interpreter for an even broader audience. Average effects became selfish genes and individuals became lumbering robots controlled by their genes. Group selection became a pariah concept, taught only as an example of how not to think. As one eminent evolutionist advised a student in the 1980s, 'There are three ideas that you do not invoke in biology: Lamarkism, the phlogistron theory, and group selection.'

Scientific dogmatism

In retrospect, it is hard to fathom the zeal with which evolutionists such as Williams and Dawkins rejected group selection and developed a view of evolution as based entirely on self-interest. Williams ended *Adaptation and Natural Selection* with the phrase 'I believe that it is the light and the way.' Here is how Dawkins recounts the period in his 1982 book *The Extended Phenotype*:[164]

> The intervening years since Darwin have seen an astonishing retreat from his individual-centered stand, a lapse into sloppily unconscious group-selectionism . . . We painfully struggled back, harassed by sniping from a Jesuitically sophisticated and dedicated neo-group-selectionist rearguard, until we finally regained Darwin's ground, the position that I am characterizing by the label 'the selfish organism . . .

This passage has all the earmarks of fundamentalist rhetoric, including appropriating the deity (Darwin) for one's own cause. Never mind that Darwin was the first group selectionist. Moreover, unlike *The Selfish Gene*, *The Extended Phenotype* was written by Dawkins for his scientific peers, not for a popular audience!

In reality, the case against group selection began to unravel almost immediately after the publication of *Adaptation and Natural Selection*, although it was difficult to tell, given the repressive social climate. In the first place, calling genes 'replicators' and 'the fundamental unit of selection' is no argument at all against group selection. The question has always been whether genes can evolve by virtue of benefiting whole groups and despite being selectively disadvantageous within groups. When this happens, the gene favoured by between-group selection replaces the gene favoured by within-group selection in the total population. In the parlance of population genetics theory, it has the highest average effect. Re-labelling the gene selfish, just because it evolves, contributes nothing. The 'gene's eye view' of evolution can be insightful in some respects, but as an argument against group selection it is one of the greatest cases of comparing apples with oranges in the annals of evolutionary thought.

The same goes for the concept of extended phenotypes, which notes that genes have effects that extend beyond the bodies of individual organisms. Examples of extended phenotypes include a bird's nest or a beaver's dam. But there is a difference between these two examples; the nest benefits only the individual builder, whereas the dam benefits all of the beavers in the pond, including those who don't contribute to building the dam. The problem of within-group selection is present in the dam example and the concept of extended phenotypes does nothing to solve it. More apples and oranges.

The revival of group selection

Much has happened in the four decades following the rejection of group selection in the 1960s. Naïve groupism is still a mistake that needs to be avoided, but between-group selection can no longer be categorically rejected. Claims for group selection must be evaluated on a case-by-case basis, along with the other major evolutionary hypotheses. Demonstrations of group selection appear regularly in the top scientific journals.

As one example reported in the 6 July 2006 issue of *Nature*,[165] a group of microbiologists headed by Benjamin Kerr cultured bacteria (*E. coli*) and their viral predator (phage) in 96-well plates, which are commonly used for automated chemical analysis. Each well was an isolated group of predators and their prey. Within each well, natural selection favoured the most rapacious viral strains, but these strains tended to drive their prey, and therefore themselves, extinct. More prudent viral strains were vulnerable to replacement by the rapacious strains within each well, but as groups they persisted longer and were more likely to colonize other wells. Migration between wells was accomplished by robotically controlled pipettes. Biologically plausible migration rates enabled the prudent viral strains to persist in the total population, despite their selective disadvantage within groups.

As a second example reported in the 8 December 2006 issue of *Science*, economist Samuel Bowles estimated that between-group selection was strong enough to promote the genetic evolution of altruism in our own species, exactly as envisioned by Darwin. These and many other examples, which Edward O. Wilson and I summarize in a review article,[166] are ignored entirely by Dawkins, who continues to recite his mantra that the selective disadvantage of altruism within groups poses an insuperable problem for between-group selection.

Individuals as groups

Not only can group selection be a significant evolutionary force, it can sometimes even be the dominating evolutionary force. One of the most important advances in evolutionary biology is a concept called major transitions. It turns out that evolution takes place not only by small mutational change, but also by social groups and multi-species communities becoming so integrated that they become higher-level organisms in their own right. The cell biologist Lynn Margulis proposed this concept in the 1970s to explain the evolution of nucleated cells as symbiotic communities of bacterial cells.[167] The concept was then generalized to explain other major transitions, from the origin of life as communities of cooperating molecular reactions, to multicellular organisms and social insect colonies.

In each case, the balance between levels of selection is not fixed but can itself evolve. A major transition occurs when selection within groups is suppressed, making it difficult for selfish elements to evolve at the expense of other members of their own groups. Selection among groups becomes a dominating evolutionary force, turning the groups into super-organisms. Ironically, during the Age of Individualism it became taboo to think about groups as organisms, but now it turns out that organisms are literally the groups of past ages.

Dawkins fully accepts the concept of major transitions, but he pretends that it doesn't require a revision in his ideas about group selection. Most important, he doesn't pose the question that is most relevant to the study of religion: Is it possible that human genetic and cultural evolution represents the newest example of a major transition, converting human groups into the equivalent of bodies and beehives?

Selfish memes and other theories of cultural evolution

Dawkins' third claim to fame, in addition to selfish genes and extended phenotypes, was to coin the term 'meme' to think about cultural evolution. In its most general usage, the word 'meme' becomes newspeak for 'culture' without adding anything new. More specific usages suggest a variety of interesting possibilities; that culture can be broken into atomistic bits like genes, that these bits are somehow represented inside the head, and especially that they can evolve to be organisms in their own right, often spreading at the expense of their human hosts, like the demons of old.

As with religion, Dawkins has not conducted empirical research on cultural evolution, preferring to play the role of Mycroft Holmes, who sat in his armchair and let his younger brother Sherlock do the legwork. Two evolutionary Sherlocks of culture are Peter Richerson and Robert Boyd, authors of *Not By Genes Alone: How Culture Transformed Human Evolution.*[168] One of the sleights of hand performed by Dawkins in *The God Delusion*, which takes a practised eye to detect, is to first dismiss group selection and then to respectfully cite the work of Richerson and Boyd without mentioning that their theory of cultural evolution is all about group selection.

Consider genetic evolution by itself. When a new mutation arises, the total population consists of one group with a single mutant and many groups with no mutants. There is not much variation among groups in this scenario for group selection to act upon. Now imagine a species that has the ability to socially transmit information. A new cultural mutation can rapidly spread to everyone in the same group, resulting in one group that is very different from the other groups in the total population. This is one way that culture can radically shift the balance between levels of selection in favour of group selection. Add to this the ability to monitor the behaviour of others, communicate social transgressions through gossip, and easily punish or exclude transgressors at low cost to the punishers, and it becomes clear that human evolution represents a whole new ball game as far as group selection is concerned.

In this context, the human major transition probably began early in the evolution of our lineage, resulting in a genetically evolved psychological architecture that enables us to spontaneously cooperate in small face-to-face groups. As the great social theorist Alexis de Tocqueville commented long ago in *Democracy in America*, 'the village or township is the only association which is so perfectly natural that, wherever a number of men are collected, it seems to constitute itself.' As the primate equivalent of a beehive or an ant colony, our lineage was able to eliminate less groupish competitors. The ability to acquire and socially transmit new behaviour enabled our ancestors to spread over the globe, occupying hundreds of ecological niches. Then the invention of agriculture enabled group sizes to increase by many orders of magnitude, but only through the cultural evolution of mechanisms that enable groups to hang together at such a large scale. Defining, motivating, coordinating and policing groups is not easy at any scale. It requires an elaborate system of proximate mechanisms, something akin to the physiological mechanisms of an individual organism. Might the elements of religion be part of the 'social physiology' of the human group organism? Other than briefly acknowledging the abstract possibility that memes can form 'memeplexes,' this possibility does not appear in Dawkins' analysis.

Bring on the legwork

It is absurd, in retrospect, that evolutionists have spent much more time evaluating the major evolutionary hypotheses for guppy spots than for the elements of religion. This situation is beginning to remedy itself as scholars and scientists from all backgrounds begin to adopt the evolutionary perspective in their study of religion.

An example from my own research will show how empirical legwork can take us beyond armchair theorizing. Here is Dawkins on the subject of whether religion relieves or induces stress in the mind of the religious believer.[169]

> Is religion a placebo that prolongs life by reducing stress? Possibly, although the theory must run the gauntlet of skeptics who point out the many circumstances in which religion causes rather than relieves stress . . . The American comedian Cathy Ladman observes that 'All religions are the same: religion is basically guilt, with different holidays.'

One of my projects is a collaboration with the psychologist Mihaly Csikszentmihalyi (pronounced shick-sent-me-hi), who is best known among general readers for his books on peak psychological experience, such as *Flow* and *The Evolving Self*.[170] Csikszentmihalyi pioneered the Experience Sampling Method (ESM) which involves signalling people at random times during the day, prompting them to record their external and internal experience – where they are, who they are with, what they are doing, and what they are thinking and feeling on a checklist of numerical scales. The ESM is like an invisible observer, following people around as they go about their daily lives. It is as close as psychological research gets to the careful field studies that evolutionary biologists are accustomed to performing on non-human species, which is why I teamed up with Csikszentmihalyi[171] to analyse some of his past studies from an evolutionary perspective.

These studies were performed on such a massive scale and with so much background information that we can compare the psychological experience of religious believers versus non-believers on a moment-by-moment basis. We can even compare members of conservative versus liberal protestant denominations, when they are alone versus in the company of other people. On average, religious believers are more prosocial than non-believers, feel better about themselves, use their time more constructively and engage in long-term planning rather than gratifying their impulsive desires. On a moment-by-moment basis, they report being more happy, active, sociable, involved and excited. Some of these differences remain even when religious and non-religious believers are matched for their degree of prosociality. More fine-grained comparisons reveal fascinating differences between liberal versus conservative protestant denominations, with more anxiety among the liberals and conservatives feeling better in the company of others than when alone. Religions are diverse, in the same way that species in ecosystems are diverse. Rather than issuing monolithic statements about religion, evolutionists need to explain religious diversity in the same way that they explain biological diversity.

These results raise as many questions as they answer. We did not evolve to feel good but rather to survive and reproduce. Perhaps religious believers are happily unaware of the problems that non-believers are anxiously trying to solve. As a more subtle point, people pass back and forth between the categories of 'non-believer' and 'believer' as they lose and regain faith. Perhaps some non-believers are psychologically impaired because they are the recent casualties of religious belief. Only more scientific legwork can resolve these issues, but one thing is sure: Dawkins' armchair speculation about the guilt-inducing effects of religion doesn't even get him to first base.

Natural historians of religion

Hypothesis testing does not always require quantification and the other trappings of modern science. Darwin established his entire theory on the basis of descriptive information carefully gathered by the naturalists of his day, most of whom thought that they were studying the hand of God. This kind of information exists in abundance for religions around the world and throughout history, which should be regarded as a fossil record of cultural evolution so detailed that it puts the biological fossil record to shame. It should be possible to use this information to evaluate the major evolutionary hypotheses, which after all represent radically different conceptions of religion. Engineering principles dictate that a religion designed to benefit the whole group will be different from one designed to benefit some individuals (presumably the leaders) at the expense of others within the same group, which in turn will be different from a cultural disease organism designed to benefit itself at the expense of both individuals and groups, which in turn will be different from a religion for which the term 'design' is inappropriate. It would be odd indeed if such different conceptions of religion could not be distinguished on the basis of carefully gathered descriptive information.

Of course, it is necessary to gather the information systematically rather than picking and choosing examples that fit one's pet theory. In *Darwin's Cathedral*, I initiated a survey of religions drawn at random from the 16-volume *Encyclopedia of World Religions*, edited by the great religious scholar Mircia Eliade. The results are described in an article titled 'Testing Major Evolutionary Hypotheses about Religion with a Random Sample,' which was published in the journal *Human*

Nature and is available on my website. The beauty of random sampling is that, barring a freak sampling accident, valid conclusions for the sample apply to all of the religions in the encyclopaedia from which the sample was taken.

By my assessment, the majority of religions in the sample are centred on practical concerns, especially the definition of social groups and the regulation of social interactions within and between groups. New religious movements usually form when a constituency is not being well served by current social organizations (religious or secular) in practical terms and is better served by the new movement. The seemingly irrational and otherworldly elements of religions in the sample usually make excellent practical sense when judged by the only gold standard that matters from an evolutionary perspective — what they cause the religious believers to do. The best way to illustrate these points is by describing one of the religions in the sample – Jainism – which initially appeared the most challenging for the group-level adaptation hypothesis.

Jainism is one of the oldest and most ascetic of all the Eastern religions and is practised by approximately 3per cent of the Indian population. Jain ascetics filter the air they breathe, the water they drink and sweep the path in front of them to avoid killing any creature no matter how small. They are homeless, without possessions and sometimes even fast themselves to death by taking a vow of 'santhara' that is celebrated by the entire community. How could such a religion benefit either individuals or groups in a practical sense? It is easy to conclude from the sight of an emaciated Jain ascetic that the religion is indeed a cultural disease – until one reads the scholarly literature.

It turns out that Jain ascetics comprise a tiny fraction of the religion, whose lay members are among the wealthiest merchants in India. Throughout their long history, Jains have filled an economic niche similar to the Jews in Western Europe, Chinese in Southeast Asia and other merchant societies. In all cases, trading over long distances and plying volatile markets such as the gem trade requires a high degree of trust among trading partners, which is provided by the religion. Even the most esoteric (to outsiders) elements of the religion are not superfluous by-products but perform important practical work.

For example, the ascetics must obtain their food by begging, but their religion includes so many food restrictions that they can only accept food from the most pious lay Jain households. Moreover, the principle of non-action dictates that they can only accept small amounts of food from each household that was not prepared with the ascetics in mind. When they enter a house, they inspect the premises and subject the occupants to sharp questions about their moral purity before accepting their food. It is a mark of great honour to be visited but of great shame if the ascetics leave without food. In effect, the food begging system of the ascetics functions as an important policing mechanism for the community. This is only one of many examples, as summarized by Jainism scholar James Laidlaw in a 1995 book whose title says it all: *Riches and Renunciation: Religion, Economy, and Society Among the Jains.*

How then, is it possible to live by impossible ideals? The advantage for addressing this question to Jainism is that the problem is so very graphic there. The demands of Jain asceticism have a pretty good claim to be the most uncompromising of any enduring historical tradition: the most aggressively impractical set of injunctions which any large number of diverse families and communities has ever tried to live by. They have done so, albeit in a turbulent history of change, schism and occasionally recriminatory 'reform,' for well over two millennia. This directs our attention to the fact that yawning gaps between hope and reality are not necessarily dysfunctions of social organization, or deviations from religious systems. The fact that lay Jains make up what is – in thoroughly worldly material terms – one of the most conspicuously successful communities in India, only makes more striking and visible a question which must also arise in the case of the renouncers themselves.

This example illustrates a phenomenon that I call the transformation of the obvious. Jainism appears obviously dysfunctional based on a little information, such as the sight of an emaciated ascetic or beliefs that appear bizarre when taken out of context. The same religion becomes obviously functional based on more information. This is the kind of 'natural history' information that enabled Darwin to build such a strong case for his theory of evolution, and it can be used to build an equally strong case for the group-functional nature of Jainism. As for Jainism, so also for most of the other enduring religions of the world.

An emerging consensus?

I recently attended a conference on evolution and religion in Hawaii that provided an opportunity to assess the state of the field. It is not the case that everyone has reached a consensus on the relative importance of the major evolutionary hypotheses about religion. My own talk included a slide with the words 'SHAME ON US!' in large block letters, chiding my colleagues for failing to reach at least a rough consensus, based on information that is already at hand. This might seem discouraging, until we remember that all aspects of religion have so far received much less attention than guppy spots from an evolutionary perspective. The entire enterprise is that new.

There was, I believe, a convergence taking place during the short period of the conference. Richard Sosis, whose previous research includes a detailed comparison of religious versus non-religious communal movements, presented new research on the recitation of psalms among Israeli women in response to terrorist attacks. William Irons and several other participants developed the concept of hard-to-fake signals as a mechanism for ensuring commitment in religious groups. Dominic Johnson reminded us that inter-group conflict, as much as we might not like it and want to avoid it, has been an important selective force throughout human genetic and cultural evolution and that some elements of religion can be interpreted as adaptations for war. In my response to this paper during the question period, I largely agreed with Johnson but pointed out that most of the religions in my random sample did not spread by violent conflict (e.g. Mormonism). Johnson is currently examining the religions in my random sample in more detail with respect to warfare, a good example of cumulative, collaborative research. Peter Richerson and I gave a tutorial on group selection, which was especially useful for participants whose understanding of evolution is grounded on the Age of Individualism.

Lee Kirkpatrick delivered a lecture titled 'Religion is Not an Adaptation' that might seem to oppose the adaptationist accounts mentioned above. What he meant, however, is that he doubts the existence of any genetic adaptations that evolved specifically in a religious context. He is sympathetic to the possibility that more general genetically evolved psychological adaptations are co-opted by cultural evolution to form elaborately functional religious systems. Similarly, other psychologically oriented talks about minimal counter-intuitiveness (beliefs being memorable when they are weird but not too weird), hyperactive agent detection devices (our tendency to assume agency, even when it does not exist), and the ease with which children develop beliefs about the afterlife, might be interpretable as non-adaptive by-products, but they might also be the psychological building blocks of highly adaptive religions. In evolutionary parlance, by-products can become exaptations, which in turn can become adaptations.

No one at the conference presented a compelling example of a religious belief that spreads like a disease organism, to the detriment of both individuals and groups. The demonic meme hypothesis is a theoretical possibility, but so far it lacks compelling evidence. Much remains to be done, but it is this collective enterprise that deserves the attention of the scientific research community more than angry diatribes about the evils of religion.

Real-world solutions require a correct diagnosis of the problems

Explaining religions as primarily group-level adaptations does not make them benign in every respect. The most that group selection can do is to turn groups into super-organisms. Like organisms, super-organisms compete, prey upon each other, coexist without interacting or engage in mutualistic interactions. Sometimes they form cooperative federations that work so well that super-super-organisms emerge at an even larger spatial scale. After all, even multicellular organisms are already groups of groups of groups. In a remarkable recent book titled *War and Peace and War*, Peter Turchin analyses the broad sweep of human history as a process of cultural multi-level selection that has increased the scale of human society, with many reversals along the way – the rise and fall of empires. Religion is a large subject, but the explanatory scope of evolutionary theory is even larger.

American democracy can be regarded as a cultural super-super-organism. The founding fathers realized that religions work well for their own members but become part of the problem at a larger social scale. That is why they worked so hard to accomplish the separation of church and state, along with other checks and balances to prevent some members of the super-super-organism from benefiting at the expense of others. In this context I share Dawkins' concern that some religions are seeking to end the separation of church and state in America. I am equally concerned that the checks and balances are failing in other respects that have nothing do to with religion, such as unaccountable corporations and extreme income inequality.

I also share Dawkins' concern about other aspects of religions, even after they are understood as complex group-level adaptations. Religions can be ruthless in the way that they enforce conformity within groups. Most alarming for a scientist, religions can be wanton about distorting facts about the real world on their way towards motivating behaviours that are adaptive in the real world. We should be equally concerned about other distortions of factual reality, such as patriotic histories of nations and other non-religious ideologies that I call 'stealth religions' in my most recent book, *Evolution for Everyone.* Finally, I agree with Dawkins that religions are fair game for criticism in a pluralistic society and that the stigma associated with atheism needs to be removed. The problem with Dawkins' analysis, however, is that if he doesn't get the facts about religion right, his diagnosis of the problems and proffered solutions won't be right either. If the bump on the shark's nose is an organ, you won't get very far by thinking of it as a wart. That is why Dawkins' diatribe against religion, however well intentioned, is so deeply misinformed.

On scientific open-mindedness

Towards the end of *The God Delusion*, Dawkins waxes poetic about the open-mindedness of science compared to the closed-mindedness of religion. He describes the heart-warming example of a scientist who changed his long-held beliefs on the basis of a single lecture, rushing up to his former opponent in front of everyone and declaring 'Sir! I have been wrong all these years!'

This inspiring example represents one end of the scientific bell curve when it comes to open-mindedness. At the other end are people such as Louis Agassiz, one of the greatest biologists of Darwin's day, who for all his brilliance and learning never accepted the theory of evolution. Time will tell where Dawkins sits on the bell curve of open-mindedness concerning group selection in general and religion in particular. At the moment, he is just another angry atheist, trading on his reputation as an evolutionist and spokesperson for science to vent his personal opinions about religion.

It is time now for us to roll up our sleeves and get to work on understanding one of the most important and enigmatic aspects of the human condition.

13 Public terror versus public good

Ian Reader

Reading recent debates over whether or not religion is innately dangerous – ranging from polemicists such as Richard Dawkins, Sam Harris and Christopher Hitchens on one side,[172] to those, such as Keith Ward and Charles Kimball,[173] who view religion positively – reminds me of the Buddhist story in which blind men were asked to describe an elephant. Each grasps a part of the elephant and thinks this represents the whole; he who grasped the head said an elephant was like a pot, he who felt its leg said it was like a pillar and so on, until their conflicting views led them to blows. The story illustrates how clinging to one-dimensional perspectives is a path of ignorance that prevents full understanding, and it clearly shows the folly – irrational and unscientific – of taking one aspect of anything and treating it as the whole.

Dawkins, Harris and Hitchens have seized on just one of the multiple aspects of religion – acts of violence – and, like the blind man with the elephant's trunk, used it as a manifestation of its totality. In their rhetoric 'religion' becomes an irrational, one-dimensional, violence-inducing entity, with a mind of its own. Thus, although Hitchens refers to religion's 'man-made' nature[174] he treats it as if it were a free-standing entity with its own autonomous voice, for example when demanding that 'it' should apologize for its activities.[175] In such rhetoric there is scant comprehension of the complexities of 'religion'; Dawkins and Harris misguidedly conflate 'religion' with monotheism, while Dawkins absurdly states that he will not discuss Buddhism and Confucianism in his attacks on 'religion' since 'there is something to be said for treating these not as religions at all but as ethical systems or philosophies of life'.[176] Such simplistic misunderstanding might just have passed muster in the 19th century, when little was known about Buddhism and early secular humanists were keen to find common ground with their own thought systems, but it cannot be accepted now. As any undergraduate Religious

Studies student could tell Dawkins, while Buddhism expresses ethical systems and philosophies of life (as does Christianity, of course!) it is every bit as much of a 'religion' – with all the 'irrational' activities, such as worship of icons, tales of miracles, prayers, supplications and rituals that go with it – as the monotheistic religions that Dawkins reviles.

Almost diametrically opposed to the 'anti-religion' camp – yet almost as one-dimensional – are those scholars and theologians who defend 'religion' against arguments that it causes harm, by demonstrating – via virtually a reverse Dawkins methodology – its seemingly innate goodness. In *When Religion Becomes Evil*, Charles Kimball speaks of 'when religion becomes evil', by arguing that it is essentially good – but that it can be 'corrupted'.[177] Keith Ward views religion likewise in his book, *Is Religion Dangerous?*, where he takes pains to separate it from responsibility for unpleasant events. Thus the Crusades are in effect the 'justified defence of the Byzantine Empire against Arab and Turkish invaders',[178] while the incendiary pronouncements of Popes that gave religious blessing to them, are ignored. Kimball and Ward are more balanced than religion's critics, since they recognize that religion has been involved in dark deeds, but as an aberration, the result of external intrusion into the normally good realm of religion. They too remain among the blind, clutching their leg of the elephant.

From Japan to northwest England: Religion good and bad

The multiple manifestations of religion and its influences historically and in the present offer countless examples to back up the arguments of both religion's despisers and its apologists. Sadly, neither camp looks beyond its one-dimensional view to consider that the existence of examples both of good and bad – and much in-between – indicates a more complex picture than they have painted.

I illustrate this with two of my own research projects, one that supports the argument that 'religion is bad' and one the opposite. The first centres on Aum Shinrikyô, the Japanese religious group that carried out the 1995 Tokyo subway attack. Aum, guided by its charismatic leader Asahara Shôkô, whom it revered as the supreme guru and embodiment of 'truth', murdered (or, in its terms, 'transformed') opponents and dissident members while accumulating weapons with which to fight a final cosmic war. This notion of cosmic war was grounded in Aum's apocalyptic visions in which it viewed the world as polarized between the forces of good and evil which would eventually confront each other in a final war, in which Aum, fighting for good, would destroy evil and transform the world into an earthly utopia. This was its sacred mission, for which devotees pledged to fight both spiritually and, eventually, physically.

Initially Aum was idealistic, trenchantly criticizing contemporary society for its materialist values and positing a spiritually enlightened alternative. However, as its warnings of an impending apocalypse failed to have much effect, it became increasingly alienated and hostile to society, and became convinced that it had to confront the 'enemies of truth'. As it did, it became increasingly violent, enhanced by its religious views that told devotees that they were more spiritually advanced and hence morally superior to ordinary humans – they were 'permitted' to transcend normal moralities in advancing their cause. Indeed, the very act of killing became a morally righteous and mystical deed in the eyes of devotees; being selected as a 'sacred warrior' with orders to kill an enemy of 'the truth' was an indication of one's own spiritual transcendence.

In its religious orientations and beliefs in its violence, Aum is similar to several other apocalyptic movements impelled by polarized world views into confronting the world at large. Aum drew on a recurrent theme of millennial visions that is found in Christianity and Buddhism alike, and which has influenced other movements as well.[179] It is a good example of how dangerous religion can be, and how religious devotion and belief can lead to extremes of violence. It undermines the claim that religion is innately good and that when violence occurs, this is somehow because 'religion' has become warped or corrupted by other forces. Aum's religious beliefs and concerns about the nature of the world and the way things ought to be were key causes of its deeds; it was both religious and dangerous.

If Aum thus serves as further grist to the Dawkins/Hitchens mill, it also poses a problem for their belief that science and education offer the means of eradicating the malign influences of religion. Most of the key players in Aum's violence and its manufacture of chemical weapons were highly educated, with degrees, postgraduate training and professional experience in sciences and medicine; they believed that science and religion could be fused to bring about a new age of spiritually advanced humans, and they were keen to use their scientific knowledge to advance their religious agenda through the manufacture and use of nerve gases and other weapons.

My second example, from a study I participated in centred on Burnley and Blackburn in northwest England, involved a survey of schoolchildren in Year 10 (age 15) on issues relating to religion and tolerance. We surveyed children in two schools. School A was predominantly White and ethnically English, whereas School B's pupils were predominantly from Muslim families, initially from South Asia. In School A, few attended church or were interested in religion, reflecting a secular upbringing and home life among most of the children (Table 1). Almost no School A students saw religious institutions as having any influence on them, and they knew little about different religious traditions apart from what they heard at school. School B was much different: most of the pupils attended mosque regularly, were interested in religion and had had a religious upbringing (Table 1). In fact, for School B pupils, religious institutions were the second most important influence after their families, and over half learnt about other faiths at their local mosque.

The study appears to provide some support to arguments that religion can be a positive moral force in society. School B pupils, with their strong religious backgrounds, showed more respect and tolerance for others, including other ethnicities and faiths (Tables 2 and 3), with over two-thirds respecting others regardless of their religion, and over half respecting different ethnic backgrounds or classes. At School A however – predominantly secular – less than 40 per cent would respect others regardless of gender, ethnicity, religion or class. In School A, 41 per cent thought that one race was better than another,

Table 1 Students (Year 10) surveyed at two schools in northwest England.

	School A (124 surveyed) (%)	School B (159 surveyed) (%)
Attended religious institution (e.g. church/ mosque) regularly	8	81
Interested in religion	13	91
Had some form of religious upbringing	16	96
Never followed any religious rules	87	6

Table 2 Student replies on whether it is 'important to respect others regardless of . . .'

	School A (%)	School B (%)
Religion	30	69
Class	26	52
Gender	39	47
Ethnicity	32	54

Table 3 Student replies.

	School A (%)	School B (%)
One race better than another	41	17
Important to be friendly with those from different ethnic/religious groups	43	76
Willing to listen to others' religious views	50	86

compared to only 17 per cent in School B. In School A, barely half the pupils considered it important to be friendly with people from other religious or ethnic groups, or listen to other people's religious views; whereas over three-quarters of the School B pupils saw these forms of tolerance as important.

It was School B, then, with its stronger ethnic and religious base, that had more liberal values, community cohesion, tolerance and openness to others' religious views, and friendships between different faiths. The relatively secular pupils at School A held comparatively intolerant and racist orientations.[180] Keith Ward (2007:161–163) has also argued, based on US surveys showing more altruism and voluntary work among people with religious beliefs, that religion provides moral and social values. It might seem that a religious upbringing enhances liberal attitudes, rather than damages them, and that secular backgrounds may produce intolerance. Of course, even hard-wired despisers of religion such as Dawkins and Hitchens, do not deny that religious traditions and communities can foster moral values. They do, however, suggest that a secular religion-less world, based in rationality and science can equally foster such values – though this claim appears to be more a testimony of faith as with Hitchens' claim that 'we believe ethical life can be lived without religion' (*God is not Great*, p. 6), than an argument based on empirical data.

The problem is that, given that we do not live in a religion-free world, it is difficult to provide hard evidence that secular upbringings and societies free of religion will be able to fulfil such roles. Attempts to eradicate religion – from the French revolutionaries of the 1790s through to Stalinist Russia and Pol Pot's Cambodia – did not exactly produce more moral societies. Without empirical evidence, such claims remain unscientific and methodologically unsound. Even those who criticize religion from a scientific rationalist perspective occasionally lapse into irrational faith when promoting the things they believe in.

What data we have suggests that religion can make people more attuned to civilized values and tolerance than those without religious backgrounds. It certainly raises questions about Hitchens' claim that 'if religious instruction were not allowed until the child attained the age of reason we would be living in quite a different world' (p. 220). Sadly, if the Burnley data are anything to go by, that world might be more intolerant and racist than it is at present.

Concluding comments

I have drawn on just two of my own research experiences, but I could have cited many other examples of religious groups either doing bad things – financial scandals, manipulation of followers, violence – or doing good deeds like catering for the neglected and disabled, such as Japanese Buddhist temples that have established, with donations from pilgrims, leprosy sanatoria in impoverished areas such as Burma. If I wanted to be another blind man misrepresenting the elephant, I could project any one of these as an exemplar of the whole. But like the arguments of apologists and despisers alike, such one-dimensionality would be methodologically flawed, unscientific and irrational.

The problem is that religion is not an entity that can be isolated as a 'germ', held to blame for all manner of ills, and then eradicated; nor is it a source of inerrant good that can be kept pure and pristine. It simply – as my contrasting examples indicate – cannot be categorized in black and white. While wildly irrational apocalyptic religious groups such as Aum might make such polarized value judgements, it really is not good enough for supposedly rational academics.

Everything we refer to as or associate with 'religion' – from sacred texts to frameworks of belief, modes of worship and forms of practice – is part of the human realm, just as is, for example, politics. Whenever we try to categorize human behaviour and social organization, we cannot neatly separate out other aspects of human behaviour. 'Religion' is imbued with all the varying capacities, traits and ambivalences of the human world; as the Aum and Burnley cases show us, it can be a dangerous, irrational, intolerant threat to civilized life – and a force for tolerance, understanding and civilized values.

The cases in effect manifest two legs (but not the whole) of the metaphorical elephant of 'religion' – from the intolerant, violent and zealous, to the benign, ethically upright and compassionate. Because of its human nature, religion is morally neutral, reflecting those who shape it; it is neither intrinsically 'good' nor 'bad' although it can be both or either, as well as many other shades in between.[181] It is vital to recognize these multidimensional aspects if we are to properly discuss 'religion' as a category of analysis. Otherwise, we reduce it to a simplistic unscientific and irrational one-dimensionality, demean the subject and remain like the blind men feebly grasping different bits of the elephant's body and coming to blows over their complementary yet contradictory misunderstandings of the whole.

14 Buddhism: Is there better balance in the East?

Hiroko Kawanami

When I am confronted with a big question such as, 'is religion harmful for society?' the best I can do is to draw some insight from the wisdom of a religious tradition I am most familiar with, which is Buddhism. This concept of 'religion' differs from a theistic tradition such as Christianity or Islam, in that 'society', rather than 'God', is the focus of discussion. Debate in the West assumes faith to be practised internally – no longer a social experience. Fewer and fewer people go to church, or take part in religious activities that were once celebrated communally. Encroaching secularization has also made religion increasingly more private, depriving it of any social underpinning it used to have.

In many Asian countries, Buddhist faith is still manifested in the public arena; it does not profess to a theistic god, and is very much about the common good. It is essential in directing and shaping public opinions, and provides an ethical framework for societal well-being. The older school of Theravāda Buddhism focuses on discipline and morality. Personal and social problems are caused by ignorant humans who lack control and wisdom, and so it is not *religion* that is harmful, but *human nature* (Ian Reader makes this point in Chapter 13).

In the ancient *Aggañña Sutta*, normally translated as the 'Book of Genesis',[182] the Buddha was not a creator, but came into a world created by Brahmā. Widely used by monks in sermons, this Buddhist version of human social evolution comprises a dialogue between the Buddha and his two Brahman disciples. The Buddha disputed the Brahmans' claims of moral superiority (as born from the breath of Brahmā) by explaining the origins of human through common ancestry. In the beginning, the world was in total darkness, and sexless beings without solidity fed on the savoury Earth. These ancestors of humans were inherently greedy, and their fall happened the moment craving entered them.

Craving begat evolution, and distinctions emerged between Sun and Moon, night and day, and the well-fed and not well-fed. From this utopian, savoury world of undifferentiated beings, plants evolved, and people differentiated through vanity, pride and envy. Sexual distinction led to passion and desire for procreation. The gap between haves and have-nots widened with competition for food, which was hoarded rather than shared or distributed. The human propensity for private ownership led to more greed, and more hoarding. In other words, *craving* gave rise to social distinction, private ownership, which in turn led to more hoarding, stealing, lying and shortage of food. As people attacked each other and social disorder peaked, people got together to select a leader: *Mahā Sammata* (the Great Elect).

In this story, kingship in the Buddhist tradition was established due to the flaws of humankind, and a leader was chosen to gain control over human failing through his supreme morality. Human evolution in Buddhism is seen as retrogression and degeneration, and since humans are ultimately selfish and greedy – if left to their own devices, they are seen to sink even further.

Figure 4 There are 40, 000 nuns in Myanmar today. They have left their families to adhere to a religious life governed by strict rules.

Buddhism involves a deeply ingrained sense of natural order, grounded in the cosmic order in the Universe. Concepts such as kingship, state, society and social hierarchy are imbued with religious values and meanings. European Enlightenment ideals are essentially absent in these countries, with little questioning of the royal and ecclesiastical power. Even after Buddhist monarchs were dethroned by colonial powers in the 19th century, kingship retains its mythical status, almost sacrosanct in popular belief. In Thailand, the monarch is the apex of society, under the ideal of *dharmaraja*: a righteous king, who embodies both moral authority and political power, and regarded almost godlike by the people. However, it was essential for him to safeguard peace and social harmony, and establish a coterminous relationship between the state and the Sangha. Monasteries and the Sangha receive royal patronage, while monks meditate on the otherworldly matter of salvation. All this has justified political power in Buddhist societies.

During the 2007 anti-government demonstrations by Buddhist monks in Burma, the moral conscience of the people was expressed

Figure 5 Monasteries are crowded on full moon days. People come to interact with monks and nuns offering them food and necessities.

though religion. Ordinary people lined the streets, forming a long chain of stretched arms to protect the demonstrating monks from retaliation from soldiers. In defiance, monks overturned their begging bowls and refused any food from the military and their families. This act, depriving them of the chance to accumulate merit, was a powerful message in a Buddhist culture, where merit-making is essential for a better rebirth. Although monks were arrested and their protests quelled, religious faith, embedded in the moral fabric of society, had threatened to destabilize an oppressive military regime.

More than 80 per cent of Burmese are Buddhists, of the older school of Theravāda tradition, which upholds monasticism as its foundation. Monks command much respect, and boys from Buddhist families spend a few weeks as novices in monasteries. Adults may become ordained even for a short period to spend their time in quiet contemplation. More than half a million monks and novices, and over 40,000 nuns, were registered with the Yangon Ministry of Religious Affairs 2007. The Sangha has historically rallied resistance, with monks prominent in political protests from colonial times in the 1930s, independence in the 1940s and the pro-democracy uprising in 1988.

Successive regimes have recognized the threat of monastic community.[183] After the 1988 pro-democracy uprising, the government has tried to both control and cajole the monks, and the Sangha has become invoked as a unifying force for the country. Since the early 1990s, the regime, claiming its traditional state role as 'protector of faith', has restored monasteries and sacred sites, handed out honorary titles to senior monks and nuns, and offered them special privileges. In other words, the government is trying hard to win back their support and harness religion for their own political objectives. The Sangha, nevertheless, has not lost its wide moral appeal, as monks remain a pressure group in a political struggle against the oppressive regime.

The actual protest was started by monks in September 2007 in the provincial Burmese town of Pakokku.[184] Since monks survive by receiving food, they have been witnessing the country's economic distress by the decreasing food intake in their begging bowls. General unrest started in the backdrop of sudden hike in fuel prices, which increased the costs of

Figure 6 A female devotee makes merit as she receives blessing from the monks after offering them cooked food.

public transport, rice and oil, causing further distress and impoverishment. Pakokku is an important centre for monastic learning, and authorities were concerned about the organized, articulate monks of large monastery schools who are fiercely loyal to their teachers. Senior monks command a large following, and so state supervision over religious matters has intensified over the decades. Currently, 47 senior monks, appointed by the state, monitor monastic schools and exams, draw up monastic policies, resolve conflicts, and supervise the activities of monks and nuns. Nonetheless, they are also abbots of large monastery schools, private without state interference, supported by a vast number of monk students. During the recent protests, these senior monks remained resolutely silent despite repeated requests from the authorities to interfere, which signalled the junior monks that their teachers condoned their political engagement. Although it may appear that senior monks compromised their position in the state monastic policy, they remained autonomous and authoritative dealing with the crisis, keeping them above political turbulence without compromising their moral position stipulated in the *Vinaya*.[185]

The vast number of religious mendicants, however, may appear anachronistic to Westerners accustomed to modern, secular civil life, with its legal system, free information on the internet, independent media, social welfare, efficient police force, and so on. In Burma, however, amidst a vacuum of social and legal infrastructure, censored speech and curtailed freedom, religious institutions work as a kind of vehicle for the people. Moreover, the boundary between the laity and the monastic community is permeable since religion informs every aspect of society. For advice and leadership, people look up to monastic members, who are educated and disciplined, and they are also seen as non-partisan with a combined spirit of independence and compassion.

I have often seen monks voicing their views and representing the frustrations and sentiments of the people. I once witnessed a large fire in Mandalay where, in the midst of chaos and total confusion, with no one knowing which direction to run or what to do, monks patrolled the street to keep looters at bay. Their actions were spontaneous but authoritative, and in the absence of a reliable police force or organized fire fighters, they were the vigilantes keeping order until calm was restored. To my surprise, I remember many monks armed with batons and primitive weapons, but their presence on the streets was reassuring for many.

Religion in traditional societies cannot be understood in a civil society, where we argue sitting comfortably without fear of persecution, hunger or oppression. In the modern history of Southeast Asia, Buddhism has provided the people with a national identity, a specific world view, cosmology, an ethical code of conduct and it continues to offer them a sense of common heritage and belonging. It also can restore social stability, justice and peace. In many countries in Southeast Asia, religion has not retreated from the public arena into the private sphere. Many chants recited by Burmese monks during the recent demonstration were directed at the whole nation, sending out loving kindness and safeguarding the security of all participants. Monks are theoretically 'renouncers', which has raised discussion about their 'proper' social and religious roles. However, there is no denying their centripetal position in society for moral leadership as councillors, advisers and mediators. Monasteries have (perhaps until recently) brought people together from

Figure 7 Young boys are taken around the villages in a procession before they become initiated as novices.

different social strata, provided a safe haven for open discussions, and offered welfare services for the community. Walpola Rahula, one of the most celebrated scholarly monks in 20th-century Sri Lanka, combined leftist political orientation, socialist themes and Buddhism. He said nothing in Buddhism should prevent monks from participating in public affairs.[186] Since 'politics' includes public welfare and human activity, Rahula saw the welfare of people as a natural concern for monks, while following the *Vinaya* and its religious ideals of non-violence, wisdom and compassion.

The East may hold some insights for a troubled world, but a different religious tradition may not necessarily apply to one's own situation. In Burma, Buddhism embraces the whole way of being and expresses the moral conscience of the people. Contrary to European Enlightenment ideas – religion must be apprehended by human reason – Buddhism has advocated that intellectual reason, however advanced and developed, cannot overcome a basic human nature governed by greed, aversion and ignorance (delusion). Although the importance of enquiry is acknowledged, Buddhism teaches that reason can obstruct higher wisdom if one becomes trapped in reasoning, closing rather than opening up the mind. Human reason is regarded to be impatient, oppositional (dualistic) and inclined to have a fixed viewpoint. In Buddhism, *Enlightenment* is freedom from solipsism, self-righteousness and attachment to ego, the sources of all human suffering. Ideas and consciousness derive from sensory impressions and experiences, such that human reason is biased by the self-centred nature of our perceptions and understanding of our surrounding physical world. Concepts of autonomy, independence and rights are replaced in Buddhism by interdependence, non-self and social responsibility.

It seems to me that in the post-Enlightenment era, Western rationalists have increasingly privatized religion, and humans have become an end in themselves. The important function of religion in the past has been forgotten, and the large 'head' has come to rule the 'mind'. Meanwhile, the weight placed on rationality and science has not improved the human condition, but only enhanced belief in the omnipotence of human reasoning. Lost are qualities embodied in morality, discipline, respect for others and the notion of common good.

There has been a general misconception in the West that Buddhism has not freed people from fatalism and fear, but only allowed them to tolerate oppression, social disadvantage and accept the condition of suffering. Some even view it as a religion of nihilism, indifference and withdrawal. In a predominantly Buddhist society, however, people believe in the inter-relationship between cause and effect, that *karma* is not static, and so they work constantly to improve their karmic position by following the moral guidelines and ritual procedures to which they are unwittingly committed. Even members of the military junta are not above the natural law, since they are located within the eschatology of Buddhism and must expect karmic retribution for their brutal acts. Buddhism accepts human nature as selfish, greedy and deluded, so the imperative is to work on personal development, social engagement, wisdom and compassion and to realize the interdependent nature of human existence.

Part IV Can science itself inspire spiritual wonder? Broader views

15 Can scientific discovery be a religious experience?

John Hedley Brooke

Should scientists contest religious beliefs? One answer to this blunt question could scarcely be controversial. When religious beliefs (whatever they may be) masquerade as 'science', as in claims for a 'creation science', it seems perfectly obvious that scientists committed to the principles of neo-Darwinian evolution should have the right to retaliate and to give the reasons why Charles Darwin's theory provides a more compelling explanation for otherwise disparate natural phenomena than would recourse to independent acts of creation. Darwin brilliantly summarized those reasons in the last chapter of his *Origin of Species.* Whether belief in 'separate creation' should be called an intrinsically 'religious' belief is, however, a moot point. Certainly it is a belief sustained by a particular strand of Protestant Christianity. But it is interesting that Darwin called this model a 'theory of creation' and it is a model not required by the classical Christian doctrine of creation, which stresses the dependence of the entire Universe, and all processes within it, on a transcendent power. Another response to the question might also be relatively uncontroversial. If a particular 'religious belief' (whatever that may be) can be shown to be both ill-founded and dangerous to others, we would expect responsible people (not only scientists) to contest it. The difficulty, however, is that though we might readily produce specific examples of damaging beliefs from specific religious traditions, this is a long way from showing that there is some essence to religion that makes it the root of all evil, or indeed that in any one faith tradition there is a pre-ponderance of damaging beliefs over others that may be beneficial to those who hold them.

As soon as we start looking for difficulties with the question, they rain down on us. Behind it there lurks the notion that beliefs derived from sacred texts and from faith traditions, or held on the basis of intuition or trust, are inherently suspect compared with those for which scientists can produce empirical evidence. It is easy to forget, however, that for those who choose to live their lives *as if* something were true that might not be directly verifiable, there can be a *coherence* between what they believe and their experience, which they find life-enhancing. Notoriously, religious beliefs can reinforce unhealthy segregation, yet few would now deny their role in binding a community together, in reinforcing moral codes and in endorsing particular values. This makes it especially difficult to generalize about the propriety of attacking religious belief because one could find oneself attacking that without which particular societies would be disadvantaged not ameliorated. In Darwin's own day there was a moral revolt against certain Christian teachings, notably the belief in eternal damnation for those outside the fold. And yet there was also a powerful etiquette, which recognized that to deliberately contest the beliefs of those whose faith was precious to them was decidedly churlish.

There are deeper questions. Religions are not just about beliefs, warrantable or not. They are about practices, ranging from prayer and meditation to formalized prescriptions for group and individual behaviour. Christianity has arguably been the exception in being so creedal. Even when belief becomes the principal focus of attention there is still the problem concerning what it is that makes a religious belief 'religious'. Isaac Newton believed that the universality of the laws of nature was a consequence of the fact that the Universe and its laws were created by a single Mind. Was this a 'religious' belief? If so, to contest it would have been to pull the rug from under the metaphysics that supported his physics. To characterize religious belief as belief in supernatural agency may capture an aspect of some of the world's religions, but it is easy to overlook at least three complications. The characterization does not fit them all. Second, it fails to discriminate between a belief in 'God' or 'gods' that is purely philosophical and one that is associated with worship or other forms of piety. And third, it overlooks what for the historian of science is one of the most fascinating issues – the way in which boundaries between the natural and the supernatural have changed with time. To describe an occurrence as supernatural one has to know the limits of the natural – and it is precisely those limits that have changed with the progress of science itself. The nature/supernature dichotomy is not a timeless given.

The question is whether the experience of scientific discovery might itself, in certain circumstances, qualify as a 'religious' experience. If it can, to locate the experience in some kind of contest *between* science and religion would be incongruous. The claim that all-that-is is 'natural' goes beyond what science itself has established or possibly could establish concerning the scope of naturalistic explanation.

A mistake is often made – perhaps by scientists more than by their colleagues in the humanities – when it is asserted that the primary function of religious systems is explanatory. When it becomes so, the risk of a territorial struggle with the sciences is magnified. This is not inconvenient for those who wish to trump the triumph of a scientific rationality. But the great religions of the world have offered something rather different – spiritual transformation, hope, resources for coping with suffering, and ways of understanding and *interpreting* (not simply explaining) human existence. It can be misguided for a scientist to contest religious beliefs if the attack is launched on the premise that religions can be reduced to sets of explanatory hypotheses. For this same reason there is also a pragmatic consideration. It may be counter-productive to insist on a general contradiction between religious beliefs and the conclusions of science. The vast majority of scientific theories are ultimately descriptive of natural processes and need not impinge on religious sensibilities. The fact that naturalistic explanations are possible for once-mysterious phenomena would not be perceived as a threat by any thinking theist, yet evangelists for atheism often assume that it should be. But more to the point, if members of the public are told they have to choose between religious beliefs embedded in their local cultures, which give meaning and orientation to their lives, and statements embedded in scientific theory, their reaction may well be to reject the latter because, however firmly corroborated, they rarely offer comparable existential solace. If the goal is to proselytise on behalf of Darwinian science, to transform it into an atheistic ideology can be to shoot oneself in the foot.

If Richard Dawkins is taken as representative, it is worth noting, however, that despite his penchant for attacking the worst features of organized religion, he has attempted to discriminate between beliefs that he cannot respect and those he considers more tolerable (see also David Sloan Wilson's Chapter 12). He has, for example, declared that while he has no respect for the idea of an intervening deity who might be supposed to hear intercessory prayer and to change what would otherwise have happened, he might bring himself to respect the God of the deists, one who set the Universe up with an initial configuration of laws and capacities that would eventually produce human beings (see Simon Coleman's Chapter 4). Not that he shares belief in that God, but Dawkins recognizes, as did Thomas Henry Huxley in the 19th century, that it is not necessarily ruled out by scientific knowledge. Darwin himself *does* appear to have held that belief at the time he wrote his *Origin of Species*, referring to 'laws impressed upon matter by the Creator' and regarding the outcomes of biological evolution as the result of 'designed laws' but with the 'details left to chance'.

Religious language in science: Darwin in 1859/60

In November 1859, on the brink of publication and eagerly anticipating the reaction of the naturalists he most respected, Darwin confided to Alfred Russel Wallace: 'If I can convert Huxley I shall be content'.[187] A month later he had apparently succeeded. To Joseph Hooker he reported that Huxley 'says he has nailed his colours to the mast, and I would sooner die than give up, so that we are in as fine a frame of mind . . . as any two religionists'.[188] Religious metaphors were useful to Darwin as he tested the reactions of those whom he wished to count as his inner circle of converts. Both playfully and not so playfully he would describe his theory as a 'damnable heresy'. After a stinging reproach from his old Cambridge friend Adam Sedgwick he deemed himself a 'martyr'. There were elements of his theory for which he chose the word 'dogma'.

Darwin is also interesting in this respect because, late in life, he wrote that the beauty he once experienced in nature had been connected in his mind with belief in God. It was during his later agnostic period that he had become anaesthetized. In 1832, when he had first tasted the sublime in nature, experienced in the luxuriance of the Brazilian rain forest, his language had something of the religious about it: 'twiners entwining twiners, tresses like hair, beautiful Lepidoptera, silence, hosanna'.[189] The progression is interesting because it invites the question whether responses to the beauty of a scientific theory, as well as to the realities such theories purport to describe, might spark religious reflection. By 'religious' here I mean having to do with a sense of the transcendent, of being in touch, however tenuously, with a reality greater than the sum of nature's forces and the mundane events that routinely shape our lives. I believe (!) there is sufficient evidence from the history of science to suggest there can indeed be a trajectory from an appreciation of beauty in creation to deeper reflections on human destiny. In propelling that suggestion there are, however, several hurdles to jump.

Two immediate complications?

Is it not the sciences, with what Keats described as their 'cold philosophy' that led to the desacralization and disenchantment of nature? Is it not the sciences, with their ever increasing scope, that have driven the gods from the world? These are commonly held assumptions, but they are not the whole truth. There is much to be said for the converse argument, recently urged by Peter Harrison,[190] that it was the disenchantment of the world that made science possible. Critically the disenchantment came largely from within religion itself, through the medium of the Protestant Reformation.

A second complication is this: whether an experience of scientific discovery is to count as a religious experience can really only be decided by the subject. It would surely be presumptuous of an outside observer to judge either way? How an experience is interpreted depends, however, on the conceptual framework of the person concerned. If the subject does not interpret the experience in religious terms, it can hardly be for others to do so. But, by the same token, we must surely then allow that when scientists with religious convictions claim to have had something akin to religious experience in their work, their own interpretation cannot simply be brushed aside. The language in which scientific discoveries are delivered to the world can be surprising and revealing.

The language of discovery

The case for pursuing the question gains strength from what Ian Ramsey (Oxford philosophy professor and former Bishop of Durham) called moments of 'disclosure' when a problem is suddenly seen in a new light. These are moments when 'the penny drops', which have been a recurring feature of the sciences. A telling example comes from Europe around 1860, when there was no unequivocal method for fixing atomic weights, and as many as 16 different formulas existed for a compound as simple as acetic acid. By the electrochemical theories of the day, the idea of polyatomic molecules was practically unthinkable since repulsion between identical atoms was thought to make them unstable (for similar reasons, Avogadro's hypothesis of some 50 years earlier – that equal volumes of gases at the same temperature and pressure would contain the same number of molecules – had yet to be accepted). Following a chemical congress held in Karlsruhe in 1860, at which Cannizzaro resuscitated a viable distinction between atom and molecule, two Russian chemists had almost identical moments of insight. Both Mendeleev and Lothar Meyer described their experience as one in which scales fell from their eyes, Meyer adding that 'doubts vanished, and a feeling of calm certainty came in their place'.

The language employed in such circumstances has sometimes been explicitly that of a conversion experience. Here is just one account, from Darwin's contemporary Alfred Newton. He is referring to that issue of the *Journal of the Linnaean Society* in which the innovative papers by Darwin and Wallace appeared together:

> Never shall I forget the impression it made upon me. Here was contained a perfectly simple solution of all the difficulties which had been troubling me for months past. I hardly know whether I at first felt more vexed at the solution not having occurred to me, than pleased that it had been found at all . . . All personal feeling apart, it came to me like the direct revelation of a higher power; and I awoke next morning with the consciousness that there was an end of all the mystery in the simple phrase, 'Natural Selection'.

Like the direct revelation of a higher power. This is the resonance with a religious experience that deserves attention. Of course, in this particular case there is an irony because the conversion is arguably from a religious to a scientific understanding. A problem therefore remains: can one not say that in the religious case a sense of mystery is heightened, whereas in a disclosure that we might call 'scientific' mystery is dispelled?

The problem of disanalogy

Standard accounts of religious experience rarely refer to the sense of awe that can come from the intense study of nature. For example, in her book *The Evidential Force of Religious Experience*, Caroline Franks Davis[191] describes the sense of a spiritual presence, which may have no equivalent in science. The union of the mystic with a transcendent 'Other' is also absent from the scientific quest. There might just be an analogy between the 'dying to oneself' of the mystic and the renunciation of subjectivity (i.e. objectivity) in traditional ideologies of science, but only tenuously: the mystical case involves a renunciation of this world, whereas in science a positive embrace of the world provides mental stimulus and delight. Regenerative experiences associated with the language of salvation seem distant from what the scientist might experience in dialogue with nature. Feelings of the numinous, of being overpowered by a majestic holiness, seem not to chime with the scientist's own quest for *power over* nature. We are surely left with a fundamental disanalogy between the incomprehensibility at the heart of religious experience and the rational quest for comprehensibility epitomized by the sciences? The 'truth' for science and religion may be fundamentally different, as Simon Coleman discusses.

For all his delight in moments of disclosure, Ian Ramsey himself had to admit that religion and science have different logics of verifiability. 'God is love' could not be tested in the same manner as propositions about the workings of nature. Does this mean that our original question must be abandoned? Do these differences carry the day? Or should 'religious experience' be expanded to include the kind of revelation of which scientists sometimes speak? In fact, the scientific and the mystical are not always placed in opposition. For example, the modern physicist Frank Close was once asked to describe the most thrilling moment his research had given him. His reply was the 'first time an experiment confirmed my theory and I felt humbled by having "caught Nature at it"'. He proceeded to say the fact that Nature already 'knew'about his equations was an 'eerie and mystical experience'. It was 'an incredible surprise that quarks were for real!' And so, from the interviewer came the inevitable question: 'Do you believe in God'. To which came the conventional reply: 'not in a conventional sense'.[192]

Rapture within the sciences

From the history of science, it is possible to find many other examples of scientists whose theology may not have been conventional but who expressed a comparable rapture at having 'caught nature at it'. When the 17th-century astronomer Johannes Kepler discovered the third of his planetary laws – that the square of the orbital period is proportional to the cube of the mean diameter – he confessed to 'unutterable rapture at the divine spectacle of heavenly harmony'. That the planets of our solar system had gone into closed orbits rather than veering off tangentially confirmed Newton's belief in a deity 'very well skilled in mechanics and geometry'.

In a more recent period, physicist Werner Heisenberg spoke of the humility in which one had to accept the gift of 'an incredible degree of simplicity' in the mathematical abstractions of physical theory. These beautiful interrelationships could not be invented: in his words 'they have been there since the creation of the world'. That confidence in the very possibility of scientific discovery was once again associated with a religious reference. Heisenberg's wife records that he had once said to her: 'I was lucky enough to look over the good Lord's shoulder while he was at work.'

Striking examples are also to be found in early geology and life sciences. Here is the 19th-century Scottish evangelical Hugh Miller describing his first encounter with fossil forms: 'I was lost in admiration and astonishment, and found my very imagination paralysed by an assemblage of wonders that seemed to outrival, in the fantastic and the extravagant, even its wildest conceptions.' His own appreciation of the beauty of fossil forms was crafted into a defence of the proposition that with his Maker he shared the same aesthetic sensibilities.

As Dawkins has made clear, one can appreciate the beauty of nature and of a scientific theory without extrapolating into religious affirmation. And yet the graduation from aesthetic to theological language pervades the history of science, even among those without belief in a personal God. For Albert Einstein, the frame of mind in which great scientific discoveries were made was like that of the religious person or the person in love. For many scientists who have believed in a personal God, the discovery of elegant mechanisms in nature has usually corroborated rather than subverted a pre-existing faith. The range of emotion typically experienced by research scientists, includes this innocent testimony by the American physicist Robert Wilson:[193]

> You go through this long period of filling yourself up with as much information as you can. You just sort of feel it all rumbling around inside you . . . Then . . .you begin to feel a solution, a resolution bubbling up to your con-

> sciousness. At the same time you begin to get very excited, tremendously elated – pervaded by a fantastic sense of joy . . . But there's an aspect of terror too in these moments of creativity . . . being shaken out from your normal experience enhances your awareness of mortality.

Such experiences might not warrant the description 'religious', but the similarity in sentiment can hardly be denied. Similarly for Richard Dawkins, the plotting of planets or the unweaving of rainbows[194] may indeed generate a genuine sense of beauty and harmony. Scientific discoveries, however, are rarely described nowadays as spiritual experiences, because any slippage from aesthetic to religious discourse is viewed as a lamentable confusion. The dynamics of spiritual life are lost as a consequence.

In popular questionnaires on religious belief, those who confess to *searching* for spiritual meaning are assigned to an agnostic category, in contrast with those who may have a definite spiritual belief or church affiliation. And yet it is the questing spirit that perhaps bears the closest analogy to the scientific quest, understood as a process of enquiry rather than as a set of inviolable results.

16 Heavens above!
Old notions never die. They just incorporate.

William H. Calvin

An interesting perspective on science and religion is to imagine what would happen should the search for extraterrestrial intelligence succeed.[195] Concepts will change, and that's the most interesting part of the present exercise. Old cognitive building blocks never die – they just get reinterpreted. And so I ask:

- What makes us have spiritual instincts directed at the heavens above?
- What about spirituality's constant search for meaning, especially a holistic 'everything hangs together'?
- Do our language habits cause us to go looking for actors when we observe actions, to expect a designer when contemplating an elegant pattern in nature, such as a crystal?
- How much role do abstract metaphors play in spirituality?
- And what about the 'spark' that makes humans so special among the other animals?

I cannot imagine an ape being too concerned with the heavens above, even with watching the Moon's monthly movements. Why do we imagine our central mysteries as living somewhere in the skies?

Prehistoric scenarios can illustrate the cognitive factors at work, as discussed by Steven Mithen and Tim Taylor in Chapters 9 and 10. For a prehistoric hunter or gatherer with a home base to return to after an afternoon hauling food, getting caught out after nightfall would have been scary. In an African savanna, all of those big cats have to be somewhere, and they hunt day and night. But even half a Moon makes things better psychologically. Once people started paying attention to the Moon's monthly cycle, they could take occasional chances with staying out late. For the days leading up to the full Moon, there's lots of light after sunset. But the nights after the full Moon, there's a big difference, a dark gap between twilight and moonrise.

Now consider how they might have responded to a lunar eclipse. What is the default analogy for the Moon disappearing over the course of an hour? Something being slowly eaten. The eclipsing Moon even looks as if a bite had been taken out of it. We also tend to assume that for every action, there is an actor – and so in addition, they likely assumed an unseen actor in the heavens.

Given how useful the Moon had become, an eclipse might have been threatening, especially if you hadn't been through a number of eclipses and formed the opinion that the Moon always came back – that there was automatic resurrection after being eaten – if, of course, the actor behind the action could be persuaded.

If you don't understand a process, you try out another process that you use routinely. (In brain research, I can recall a time when the telephone switchboard was the dominant metaphor for the brain. After computers were added to our conceptual toolkit, we started talking of the brain as a computer.) Everybody knows, no matter how poorly they understand the processes behind the weather, that social relationships can be influenced by pleading, flattery and gifts. In a drought, many people surely gave it a try.

Something like this was likely tried out for eclipses as well. Surprisingly, the eclipse offerings worked much better than any Rain Dance. Just imagine a shaman who claimed to be on speaking terms with whoever runs the heavens. The Shaman said that an eclipse was about to happen, even though no one could see anything wrong. And sure enough, a bite was taken out of the Moon later that night.

Pleading, flattery, gifts and dances – whichever was tried, it seemed to work because the bite soon went into reverse. Cause and effect. Indeed, sometimes the eclipse didn't happen at all, suggesting that your intervention had prevented it.

I like to view this shaman as being the first scientist, having backed into doing science without really understanding very much beyond a simple correlation. Some examples will show you how easy it is. (There are a dozen methods for warning of eclipses that I examine in *How the*

Shaman Stole the Moon, and all are considerably simpler than Stonehenge's methods).[196] If you can count backwards to when the last lunar eclipse occurred, you might stumble upon a simple rule: watch out for the sixth full Moon after an eclipse. You'll have half a chance of seeing another lunar eclipse if the clouds cooperate.

Solar eclipses occur only on the new Moon before or after this full Moon when a lunar eclipse is possible. They will be seen somewhere on Earth, but likely not where you happen to be. If the shaman were to try warning of a solar eclipse every 6 months, it would soon destroy whatever reputation the shaman had for being well connected.

But short-term warnings are still possible. The Sun itself is too bright to look at, even when half eclipsed, so no one notices anything until mattersw get serious. But the shaman could have easily gained an hour's warning, just by resting in the shade of a tree. Insects eat holes in leaves, so a leaf's shadow on the ground has little bright spots here and there. The spot's shape is not that of the hole but of the Sun. When the Sun is half eclipsed, the circular spot will have become a crescent. (It's like a pinhole camera producing an inverted image.)

Perhaps, lacking a leaf, the shaman crossed his fingers to make a pinhole. A crystal with many facets works nicely because it produces a series of circles on nearby dark surfaces. They turn into little crescents as a solar eclipse progresses. I like to think of the shaman as the first to wear a diamond ring, carrying the scientific instrument around all of the time.

More interesting than the technique is the psychology behind shamanism (as discussed also by Lewis Wolpert in his chapter), especially advance warnings. These methods are crude compared to what we can do with our modern understanding and modern instruments. Crude methods, after all, produce many false alarms, where no eclipse follows the warning. But observe the psychology: even when the shaman is wrong some of the time, the people would have thought that their pleading-and-gifts technique worked. Indeed, it completely prevented the eclipse on those occasions!

So how did the people come to view the shaman? Assuming the shaman kept the technique secret (and didn't use it whenever feeling hungry), they would have thought that *the shaman was on speaking terms with whomever runs the heavens.*

This would have been very good for business. The shaman's everyday activities surely involved producing placebo effects via authoritative reassurance. And who would doubt the shaman's 'Take this and you'll feel better' after such a demonstration of being well connected? Since at least a third of modern pain patients respond temporarily to a placebo drug, we might expect that, after an eclipse, the shaman's treatments became even more effective at relieving pain and anxiety.[197]

I also imagine this protoscientific shaman as advancing to become the first full-time priest, supported by the community and no longer having to hunt, gather, and prepare food in the manner of a part-time shaman. The society likely came to rely upon warnings so as to conduct appropriate rituals beforehand. But remember the fate of the two Chinese astronomers, Hsi and Ho, who failed to predict an eclipse and so failed to warn the emperor to schedule his rituals.[198]

Undoubtedly gods were postulated on many other occasions, but here's one that seems both powerful and approachable. So the psychology of eclipse predictions offers at least one plausible historical possibility for our preoccupation with the heavens, one that likely carries over to SETI.

Intellect is only the frosting on the deeper currents of instinct and tradition, many of which influence spiritual concerns by providing a focus around which to organize beneficial nonheavenly concerns. There's probably a more primitive undercurrent of expecting gods to be running things from a distance, somewhere out there.

What about our constant search for 'meaning', especially a holistic 'everything hangs together'? That aspect of spirituality is surely going to be a component of the public's reaction to Contact. Unless we understand something about human instinct in this area, we are going to make some serious mistakes in dealing with the Earth-bound public.

'Given our routine search for meaning, it is not surprising that religious concepts arose', I said earlier, and 'they will change as we understand brains and evolution better.'

We search for meaning quite routinely. When a person approaches, we ask ourselves 'What does he want?' When a sound stream arrives, we try to figure out the news about who did what to whom. The neurologist Adam Zeman noted[199] that a search for meaning is intertwined with most sensory input.

'Eye and brain run ahead of the evidence, making the most of inadequate information – and, unusually, get the answer wrong . . . Our knowledge of the world pervades perception: we are always seeking after meaning. Try not deciphering a road sign, or erasing the face of the man in the Moon. What we see resonates in the memory of what we have seen; new experience always percolates through old, leaving a hint of its flavour as it passes. We live, in this sense, in a 'remembered present.'

It is language that gives our search for meaning most of its daily exercise. There is nothing spiritual about most of it. Any single word is likely to be ambiguous because it has multiple connotations. Its context is needed to guide us to the intended meaning. With two words, there is more ambiguity to resolve. Worse, a group of words often refers to a unique, never-happened-before situation. (The meaning that the speaker had in mind was perhaps a set of relationships such as 'Who did what to whom.')

As listeners, our task is to guess what was in the speaker's mind. Often we can do it without any words at all, just the other's direction of gaze, posture and facial expression are enough. To that we can add a set of clues contained in a set of sounds or gestures. Encountering an action term, we go looking for an actor to go with the verb. 'Give' causes us to search for three nouns: a likely giver, the probable recipient and an object that is suitable for giving.

A word can also be abstract, a concept where you cannot point at anything. (Say, the word 'nothing'.) In sentences, the speaker may cue you about the intended level of abstractness by saying 'a dog' (the whole class of mongrels and breeds) or 'the dog' (a specific dog; you're supposed to know which one from a prior sentence). If it's 'a dog' that you hear, you automatically ignore the colour, height, hair length and disposition that make an individual dog unique. From this you get the abstract dog. All this goes under the heading of syntax and grammar. Such pointers are often omitted, leaving you to try out a range of interpretations, from the concrete to the abstract. There are lots of ways to be wrong, and speakers are expected to package the concepts well enough so that the intended listener can guess the overall meaning.

We are surprisingly comfortable with abstractions, and that makes spirituality possible. The problem, of course, is that the ambiguity load can soar, making your quality control slow. For some attributions, you may even give up and just accept what others say it means.

The quality-control problem is even worse for the speaker, who has to initially generate some options for what to say next. If it is not a matter of choosing between set pieces, it likely involves novel combinations of words. Since most of our ideas start off as incoherent as our night-time dreams (with people, places and occasions that do not go together very well), we first have to improve them.

Next, we must choose among leading candidates. If the sentence is longer than three words, we'll need to introduce syntax in the form of appropriate tags and pointers to prevent terminal ambiguity. Checking them against the 'rules' of the local syntax is much like playing a game that has arbitrary rules. To help others read your mind, you've got to make sure that your words all hang together.

We are always searching for coherence, trying to shape up combinations that 'hang together' well enough to act on. Guessing well, as we try to make a coherent story out of fragments, is routine in making and understanding sentences. It is routine when deciding what to do next.

When our quality control falters and incoherence is the best thing we can come up with, others will suspect we are dreaming or drunk. If the behaviour persists, observers may suspect hallucination, delusion or dementia.

The search for meaning permits us to pyramid complexity and nest sentences inside other sentences. We can chain meanings and call it logic if it survives double-checking. We can play formal games, checking our candidate move against the arbitrary rules. We can create contingent plans and tell good stories.

We also search for coherence in our surroundings, ways in which things unexpectedly hang together – and the pleasure we get from finding hidden patterns is striking. We have that eureka feeling each time we discover order amidst seeming chaos. This is what makes jigsaw and crossword puzzles so attractive, not to mention doing science. Spirituality is, in part, about seeking how things all hang together. Coherence finding has spawned an enormous range of art and technology.

Sometimes you don't notice an overall incoherence because short segments of it are, by themselves, understandable. You can also start a sentence with one concept and, via a familiar chain of inference, reach a conclusion that is only another way of stating the initial concept, a mere synonym. No value was added by the chain of reasoning, but you feel as if you have accomplished something, it sounds so good. 'Wherever you go, there you are.' Your luggage, of course, is another story.

There are a lot of beginners' errors to discover, the task of a lifetime. Without critical thinking, we can easily get trapped, either by our own errors or via a moneymaking trap set by another mind. We routinely see connections that aren't really there, as in astrology. We see one true connection (bleeding the patient really does help, provided that the patient has an iron accumulation disorder) and generalize it too far (bleeding all patients for whatever ails them). It can take centuries to overcome these errors.

In the aftermath of the discovery of an extraterrestrial intelligence, we'll be making mistakes like that. We can't expect the public to practice critical thinking on such short notice.

A spiritual instinct probably arose out of some predecessor instincts. Certainly sharing has to be a candidate for one of those instincts because it can be seen as leading to the Golden Rule and similar sentiments expressed in many religions.

A big ape does not simply plunder a tasty resource in another's possession, as there seems to be an innate concept of ownership via possession. An adult holding a branch may tolerate another removing some leaves, especially (in chimpanzees at least) if recently groomed by that individual. Chimpanzees occasionally hunt and the possessor of part of the carcass may share some scraps of fresh meat. This is not a matter of offering some to others. Scraps are usually shared reluctantly, and only if someone holds out an upturned palm and screeches loudly enough. If any violence occurs, it's never from the have-nots: occasionally the possessor will drive off one obnoxious beggar.[200]

Note that the chimp's prey (monkeys, bush pigs) are small. The possessor could consume the whole thing in a few hours and probably would except for interruptions by the noisy crowd with outstretched hands. But once our ancestors finally figured out how to acquire a large grazing animal about 2.5 million years ago, such an animal is simply too big to eat by yourself. Better to share and expect others to do so.

The problem is that everyone loves something that is 'free'. And so we spend a lot of time guarding against freeloaders. We even label them 'cheaters'. There seems to be an instinctual tendency to 'pay back' violators even at considerable cost to yourself, against all notions of 'economic man' looking out for Number One. This instinct, while crude, was useful to evolve our extensive tendencies to share food and help others. But it too has a dark side, such as suicide bombers who seem willing to 'pay back violators' at extreme cost to themselves.

I used to contrast all of the religious wars fought throughout history with all of the undoubted good that religions do (though now an atheist, I was brought up singing in the church choir and am quite aware of their good works and their civilizing influence on the young). But now that I know a little more about the psychology of intolerance and the history of warfare, I am less inclined to blame the religious instinct for the wars and inquisitions. My reasons seem relevant to the possible responses to a successful E.T. search.

People just naturally form up teams, ones with almost random membership. It's very handy in natural disasters, the way ad hoc search teams will form up to search collapsed buildings and rescue survivors.[201]

Membership on other teams can be equally arbitrary, as when based on what external abstraction you support. Occasionally football fan clubs beat up on one another but, then, so do their proxies. Or the group may form up around some more visible attribute, such as ethnicity or skin colour or style of haircut. I'm beginning to feel that, if they didn't organize around religious differences, they'd just organize around something else, likely without the same kind of redeeming qualities we often get from religions.

So teams will form up around how to interpret the contact. Some will suspect the science because they suspect scientists of being against spirituality. Scientists sometimes needlessly offend conservative religious people over their beliefs. Usually our sceptical response is not to the beliefs themselves but to the reasoning offered for those beliefs. The scientists usually aren't doing it to offend or because they are against spirituality. (After all, we scientists spend much of our time seeking to understand how everything hangs together and how it came to be that way.)

Scientists just automatically carry over their effective scientific argumentation techniques to reasoning about the world more generally. Wishful thinking and faulty logic seems to be everywhere (certainly in science), so why not religion as well? (The physicist Gregory Benford throws 'The Church of the Unwarranted Assumption' into one of his novels about a space colony.) Scientists automatically form up an opposing team whenever a new fact or insight is claimed. We eagerly try to prove it wrong, to find the holes in the argument – and if all that fails, we may try to show that the idea isn't even original.

Uncomfortable as this procedure may be, it is how we discover our errors and move on. A scientist (if wanting to keep his reputation as a scientist) doesn't challenge another to a duel or file a lawsuit. Or even picket his lecture.

Why should religious authorities be free of error? While some still claim special pipelines, my experience with theologians interested in science has been positive. Most differences need not get in the way of a broad cooperation on most fronts. And we will need to do a lot of consulting and cooperating in the turbulent post-contact period.

Finally, what about that 'spark' which makes humans so special among the animals? There is indeed a gap that separates humans from our ancestors and from our cousins among the great apes.[202] If we encounter an extraterrestrial intelligence, we might get a second take on the issue.

The nature of the ancestral leap to intellect and creativity has been debated for several centuries. It looks as if a big jump in intellectual capacity occurred quite recently, about 50,000 years ago, as Steven Mithen discusses. Yet we became *Homo sapiens*, big brain and all, about 200,000 years ago.[203]

That means that there was a period, lasting about 6,000 generations, when we looked human but didn't behave anything like the people of the most recent 2,000 generations. These look-alike ancestors were either intensely conservative or not very creative. For example, they might have been able to understand novel sentences spoken by the few who could create them, but without themselves being very creative. Their coherence-finding perhaps wasn't yet good enough to start from scratch.

This step up – often called 'The Mind's Big Bang' though 'The Creative Explosion' is a more informative name[204] – is not about brain size *per se.* That is a surprise. From the comparative studies of brain size spanning many species, we thought that the march in brain size (normalized to a standard body size) was what was behind human intelligence. Part of it, perhaps, but not the burst of creativity that showed up about 50,000 years ago in long-range trading, necklaces, bone tools, very fine engraving tools, portable art and those scenes painted on cave walls – see Chapter 9 by Steven Mithen and Chapter 10 by Timothy Taylor.

How did our brains change, back then? Nothing makes a good analogy, but it may be something like a hard-working computer getting an improved operating system to coordinate the old hardware. The 'upgrade' was more capable of handling long sentences, what with their demands for structuring via syntax to minimize the ambiguity, what with their need to seek coherence amid seeming chaos. That in turn made it possible to speculate about the future (including one's own death) and see trends in the past.

That upgrade likely affected spiritual practices as well, allowing them to go beyond emotional rituals and into the realm of explanations.

Without this big step, we wouldn't be thinking about SETI (see Seth Shostak's Chapter 17) and imagining the reactions here on Earth.

But notice that our intellects are very recent and riddled with bugs. The fallacies in reasoning and belief serve to fill psychology texts. That's probably because 50,000 years is just not very much time for gene variation and natural selection to clean up the initial problems. We are still unimproved prototypes: *Homo sap, version 0.8.*

So if we face the aliens any time soon, we will be hindered by our old, unresolved problems in our mental makeup. Furthermore, since any technology we encounter that is more than 50 years ahead of ours will seem like magic to us, we will be feeling bewildered. Let us hope that we have a long time after contact before having to make any serious decisions.

17 Other intelligences

Seth Shostak

There is a general perception among members of the public that astronomers have special insight into theological questions. Among the routine interrogatories that are put to me after any presentation – questions as common as the posers about black holes, the Big Bang, and the chance that aliens are roaming the globe in search of new victims for their unsavoury molestations – are queries about my religious beliefs. This is a common enough occurrence that it no longer surprises me, but I remain perplexed about the motivation.

Could it be that this is simply a response to the fact that God is often envisioned to be 'up in the sky'? Perhaps people assume that since astronomers and the Deity share the same playground, the former have some familiarity with the latter? Or is it because of the interest in, and theological relevance of, my day job: the search for extraterrestrial life – and in particular, that privileged form of biology known as 'intelligent life'? After all, self-aware, thinking beings might be competitors for God's attention and a threat to our importance.

In my experience, simply studying stars and galaxies is not a promising route to theological insight. On the other hand, finding sentient beings elsewhere might have some influence on our beliefs. Thanks to technological advance, the search for clever life is experiencing a rapid acceleration of effort (see Figure 8). New experiments could result in a discovery only a few decades from now. So it's reasonable to ask what the consequences might be, both spiritual and otherwise.

An indifferent Universe

The belief that thinking extraterrestrials exist, and that we might possibly come in contact, has waxed and waned. The Greeks envisioned many cosmi, each populated by intelligent beings – a generous,

Figure 8 Antennas of the Allen Telescope Array.

large-scale philosophy that has a trendy echo in today's concept of parallel Universes. But during most of the two millennia separating the Hellenic scholars and ourselves, the suggestion that worlds beyond Earth could house aliens was discouraged – at least in the Christian West. Such an expansive view conflicted with the notion that we have been singled out by our maker, and favoured with a visit by, and the wisdom of, his son.

This hubristic frame of reference, that *Homo sapiens* is the pinnacle of creation, was accompanied by another persistent hypothesis. For century after century, theology was considered the go-to source for knowledge of the Universe. The mindset was that religion, rather than observation, was the deciding factor in such matters as the structure of the solar system, or the surface characteristics of the Sun and Moon (assumed to be perfect, unblemished spheres). The Kantian notion that truth could be investigated by observation of the natural world was not only discouraged, but was considered an unworthy idea.

The Renaissance changed these precepts. Careful measurements of the solar system began to strongly conflict with models based on accepted theology. Within two centuries, such investigations led to an understanding of the basic science in play. Isaac Newton's physical theories generalized the earlier work of Johannes Kepler, whose laws of planetary motions relied on the accurate measures made by his predecessor and mentor, the copper-nosed Dane, Tycho Brahe. Unlike religious notions that idealized the Universe, this approach to knowledge based on observation not only begat a more satisfying understanding, but also the astounding ability to predict new phenomena. There is hardly any aspect of science that is more compelling than its power to forecast something previously unseen.

The whole, slow-motion exercise to refine our knowledge of the solar system (which, at the time, was the central habitat of the Universe) was punctuated by the work of Galileo Galilei. He converted a novelty device, the telescope, into an instrument for learning new truths, turning it on the sky and paying attention to what he saw. Galileo's views of the Moon, the Sun and Jupiter were so at odds with the more conservative teachings of the Church that he was forced by the Inquisition to recant his claims of a Sun-centred solar system, and his work was not free of residual opprobrium until a papal decree in 1992.

Why they might be out there

Both Galileo and Kepler recorded seeing things through their crude magnifying devices that renewed the speculation on alien beings, speculation that continues with increased intensity to this day. In particular, they saw 'seas' and mountains on the Moon, features (even if misinterpreted) that were so akin to earthly geography that they immediately sparked Kepler to ponder the existence of lunar inhabitants. Galileo's discovery of four moons orbiting Jupiter provoked the intriguing theological question 'why would God favour Jupiter with four satellites, if there was no one on that planet to enjoy them?' After all, our own Moon was thought to be a gift from God. Why would he bestow even greater gifts on a world without recipients?

The same idea, that space is 'wasted' if not inhabited, can be found in such modern narratives as the movie 'Contact', based on Carl Sagan's 1983 novel of the same name. It is a 'real estate' notion of God – arguing that a property isn't valuable if it isn't occupied.

Astronomical discovery of the last two centuries has greatly increased our knowledge of how much cosmic 'property' there is, and therefore strengthened the argument that we might not be alone. In 1838, Friederich Bessel was able to make the delicate measurement that revealed the distance to a star other than the Sun. He learned that 61 Cygni was more than ten light-years' distant. This was the opening salvo in an unprecedented expansion of the size of the known Universe, and it soon became general knowledge that the stars were far more remote than the imprecisely defined crystal spheres that medieval scholars thought enclosed the solar system. After Bessel, it was realized that reducing the stars to millet grains would still leave them separated by many tens of kilometres.

With the Sun and its attendant worlds no more than specks of dust in a vast, dusty arena, the idea that we are astronomically special paled. It was only natural that, at least among scientists, the belief that we are biologically or intellectually special also became suspect. It's one thing to consider that, among the few dozen large worlds of the solar system, only Earth has life. It's quite another to deny habitation to the vast realms of the stars. The modern realization that there are several hundred thousand million stars in our galaxy, and a similar number of other galaxies each with its own fleet of stars, has also intensified the argument for *intelligent* alien life. It wasn't difficult to imagine that only one planet in five housed thinking beings, as was the case before Galileo. Today, a reasonable estimate of the number of planets in a single galaxy is a million million or more. If *Homo sapiens* is the sole locus of thought in the cosmos, then what has transpired on Earth is stupefyingly improbable. And it is a tenet among astronomers that imagining you are special is nearly always a failure of imagination.

Today, with observational science ascendant and popular fiction routinely portraying a Universe stuffed with aliens, it's tempting to think that everyone has come to the conclusion that cosmic intelligence is rampant. That's not true. Academics Peter Ward and Donald Brownlee have argued that what has transpired on Earth is extremely rare, laying out their case in a recent, popular book.[205] They claim that our planet possesses peculiar properties conducive to complex life that make it virtually *sui generis.* If so, then intelligence is a scattered exception, and we might be the cleverest creatures in our galaxy, or even within a broad swath of the cosmos. That could motivate some to argue that a statistical miracle has occurred, and we are a unique (and possibly divine) construction. One cannot dismiss this idea out of hand, because we have still not found compelling evidence for *any* biology beyond Earth, either microscopic or macroscopic, dead or alive. In other words, we have yet to prove that Earth isn't the sole abode of life, let alone life of the intelligent variety.

However, there are three broad research programmes currently under way to find that proof. The first is to increase the scrutiny of our own back yard, looking for signs of biology in familiar solar system locales. These include Mars and several of the satellites of the outer solar system (e.g. the jovian Moon Europa), worlds that are strongly suspected of harbouring liquid water. Such reconnaissance could be done with sample-return missions to the Red Planet, bringing back rocks to earthly biochemists who could examine them for martian microbes, either living or fossilized. Alternatively, one might deploy robotic drilling rigs to probe the liquid ocean that is thought to underlie Europa's icy carapace.

A second effort to establish whether the dirty chemistry called life has raised its metabolic head elsewhere relies on building space-based telescopes, such as NASA's Terrestrial Planet Finder. These instruments are designed to see and analyse the light coming from planets around other stars. Should evidence for large amounts of oxygen, methane or other biogenically important compounds be discovered in their atmospheres, that would be strong evidence that life has flourished on these barely-discerned, distant worlds.

The space probes and telescopes that would make both *in situ* searches and spectroscopic analyses of planetary atmospheres possible have been on the drawing boards for years. They still await funding, but one assumes that both types of experiments will become reality within two decades.

The third scheme for finding life beyond Earth is SETI, the Search for Extraterrestrial Intelligence. SETI's premise is that technologically competent life could make its existence known with radio or light signals. Simple calculation shows that, even with modest equipment, it's possible to transmit signals across interstellar distances (and, of course, at the speed of light). SETI experiments to find emissions from other worlds have been under way since 1960, but so far have failed to book a success.

Since SETI is a long-running effort without affirmative data, many people are under the impression that the evidence for our special situation is growing: that, while simple life may yet prove to be widespread, our species might be the only conscious life in a vast, unaware Universe. However, this impression derives from a faulty understanding of the degree to which SETI researchers have examined cosmic habitats. Largely because of the lack of continuous access to large telescopes, either radio or optical, the number of star systems looked at carefully for signs of artificial signals in nearly half a century of trying is fewer than one thousand. This is a hardly a scratch on the surface of galactic inspection.

However, the rapid – indeed, exponential – increase in the speed of digital electronics is inexorably changing the landscape of SETI. New instruments, particularly the Allen Telescope Array under development in northern California, take advantage of these technological advances, and will accelerate the pace of listening efforts by orders of magnitude. Indeed, in the course of the next two dozen years, this instrument alone could examine more than a million star systems. Consequently, and despite the lack of a detected signal thus far, SETI practitioners (including me) remain sanguine about the chances for a discovery within decades.

In summary:

1. All three types of searches for extraterrestrial life will benefit from using massively improved technology in the near future, and consequently there is reason to anticipate a discovery within a generation.
2. While any life that is found in our solar system, or betrayed by the atmospheric glow of a planet around another star, will surely be

less witty than the aliens that populate TV and movies, discovery of even the dullest microbe would be of profound importance. It would be strong evidence that biology is not rare, and that the specific conditions of Earth, while singular, are not the only ones to both spawn and support life. In other words, even if all we find is microscopic company relatively nearby, we will know that life is not unusual. Indeed, coupled with the prodigious tally of planets, we might justifiably say that life is a commonplace. In such a circumstance, one might hesitate to call life 'miraculous,' just as one would risk exaggeration in calling moons or mountains 'miraculous'.

3. Most effort to discover biology elsewhere is directed to the search for simple life, on the reasonable premise that – being more common than the intelligent variety – it will be easier to find.

The implications of SETI

As noted, only SETI experiments are directly addressed to the matter of sentient life. And while finding extraterrestrial pond scum might be interesting, it's not clear that it would have implications for our religious beliefs. Finding intelligent aliens would. That fact is brutally self-evident. After all, while one might debate whether religion is an invention or a discovery, it is clearly focused on us. It is *our* species that has the ability to plan and understand, and to construct moral codes. It is the lore of mainstream religions that God has taken special pains to instruct us – not in the natural history of the Universe – but in behaviour. One presumes that this is both because we *can* be instructed and because our behaviour is important to Him. We are, in the view of some religions, 'God's children', His special charge.

Should we succeed in our quest to find other intelligences with our telescopes, doing so would clearly change the setting in which these beliefs exist. That is because the aliens would be far beyond our own level. Simply stated, any society that our instruments could detect is likely to be much more advanced than our own, at least in terms of technological development.

This is such an important statement in gauging the impact of a detection that it bears elucidation. To begin with, it is trivially true that we will not hear from civilizations that are our technological inferiors – the equivalent of alien Sumerians (or even alien Victorians). They don't broadcast.

But what about the possibility that the signal we detect comes from extraterrestrials whose command of science and technology is approximately similar to our own? While this is a common trope of science fiction, it is, in fact, highly unlikely. The reason is as follows. Our invention of radio is barely a century old. We've had the ability to transmit powerful, high-frequency signals into space for perhaps half that length of time. In other words, our 'technological lifetime' – defined by our ability for interstellar communication – is 50 or 60 years (so far). It's unclear whether we can maintain these talents deep into the future.

Technological lifetime plays a critically important role in SETI. If the average technologically competent species survives for only a few centuries or a few millennia beyond the invention of radio, then the chance that we will ever pick up a broadcast is small indeed. Alien transmissions will be like flashbulbs in a time-lapse movie of the Galaxy, popping up occasionally, but doused so quickly that at any given moment, the entire star system is dark. To some extent the severity of this problem depends on the frequency with which societies arise in the first place (how many flashbulbs fire), but it seems reasonable to conclude that finding a world populated by extraterrestrial sentients requires that the average civilization remain in a technological state for at least thousands of years.

Clearly, then, if we do find such beings, it's because they are long-lived – and have likely invented radio thousands of years ago or more. They are our technological superiors, and it's not too much to liken their likely degree of advance to the gap that separates 21st-century humans from Neanderthals.

So even if we like the idea of being God's children, we will, if a signal is found, know two important things: (1) God has other children, and (2) of the offspring we know, we're the younger. With additional detections, 'younger' will likely be replaced with 'youngest'.

In addition, of course, there's the possibility of learning something from the signal itself. Since the nearest intelligent beings are likely to be at least hundreds of light-years' distant, the senders will appreciate that – while communication across interstellar space is feasible – conversation is not. At least for biological intelligence, interchanges lasting centuries or millennia are too sluggish to be practical. Consequently, any information conveyed is a one-way transfer, much in the manner of dropping leaflets on a possibly inhabited island. If those making the broadcast have any interest in providing useful information, they will use anti-cryptographic techniques (e.g. picture dictionaries) to make their signals comprehensible, even to technical neophytes. In this way, we might be exposed to wisdom far in advance of our own. Indeed, insofar as there's any danger in the SETI enterprise, it lies herein. Could we tranquilly absorb knowledge far beyond what we have achieved on our own?

This scenario provokes speculation about the mechanism by which learning might spread, not just to us, but in a general way. It is a remarkable consequence of the physics of the cosmos that interstellar travel is exceedingly difficult – fundamentally daunted by the great distances between stars – but that sending information from star to star is relatively easy. Could it be that, having reached a level of technical sophistication that permits receiving messages from others, most cosmic intelligence is willy-nilly inducted into a 'galactic club' of advanced knowledge? If so, then humankind could very well be on the threshold of transcending the accomplishments of ten thousand generations of *Homo sapiens* by opening a door to the culture of minds that are far older than our own.

These highly speculative thoughts have surely occurred to many of our predecessors. In ancient times we turned to priests and spiritual sources for understanding. Since the Renaissance, humanists have promoted the idea that we can learn all that can be known by applying our intellect to a Universe assumed to be comprehensible. Now we are confronted with the possibility that, once again, true instruction could come from outside ourselves.

These are, without doubt, special times. As the 21st century begins, we have both sufficient knowledge and adequate technology to spot the signposts of other intelligent beings. There are no guarantees of success, but should we discover such a signal, there are two obvious questions we would hope to find answered in the bit stream discovered washing over our planet:

1. What are these other beings like?
2. Do they have religion?

Religious belief seems near-universal among societies on Earth. But could that be merely an artefact of our own construction, a device that has helped us to survive in hostile times? Is God, then, merely a fabrication of one species on a small planet in a nondescript galaxy? An answer might be found as a consequence of our quest to learn whether we are alone in the cosmos. We assume mathematics is universal, despite being a human 'invention,' and that extraterrestrials will both have mastered and understand it. Perhaps theology has a similar endemic truth. It may be that the best way to know is to ask others.

18 Natural theology in contemporary cosmology

David Wilkinson

While the legacy of Darwin demolished the design argument in the minds of biologists and theologians, the last four decades of cosmology has seen a revival of the language of design. This has been motivated by anthropic balances in the law and circumstances of the Universe, coupled with the intelligibility of the fundamental laws and the experience of awe common to scientists. Can such insights lead to a revised natural theology, which learns the lessons of the Darwinian legacy? Does the nature of the Universe at its most fundamental level lead to religious belief or evidence for an absence of God?

It is an often repeated mantra that the Darwinian controversies of the 19th century were focused on a clash between natural selection and a literal reading of the first chapter of Genesis. Thus the legacy of Darwin is often seen as the way the Christian churches had to come to terms with a non literal reading of Genesis. In fact this was not a major issue for the vast majority of Christian believers in the 19th century (see also Chapter 15 by John Hedley Brooke). In the early part of the century, geologists (many of whom were committed Christians) had shown that the Earth was far older than a few thousand years. This was not a problem for them. From the early church theologian Augustine onwards, the early chapters of Genesis had been understood in non-literal ways. John Calvin for example understood that God had accommodated his revelation of truth to the thoughts and concepts of the human mind, and that Genesis 1 was primarily concerned with who God was rather than how the Universe was made in scientific terms. In the light of this, seven day creationism, that is the belief that the Universe is only a few thousand years old, is a fairly recent 20th-century phenomenon.[206]

Far more important in challenging the religious belief of the day was the way that Darwinian evolution impacted on human uniqueness and the way that it demolished the design argument. The design argument, which argued from design in the natural world to a designer, had flourished with the growth of the scientific revolution and in the Boyle Lectures, the Bridgewater Treatises, the work of John Ray and then its classic expression in William Paley's *Natural Theology* (1802) was well set both in the academic and popular mind. Paley's classic image of walking across some land and finding a watch, so intricate in its design that you infer a designer of the watch, had become a standard way of interpreting the intricacy of the biological world. Indeed natural theology, that is the movement from evidence in the natural world to belief and description of a Creator, had replaced for many Christians the Bible in being the foundation for belief. This was in spite of aggressive attacks upon it earlier, by Immanuel Kant (1724–1804) and David Hume (1711–1776).

Darwin, gave an alternative explanation to design in the natural world. That which was thought to be special creation of God and therefore evidence of a great designer, was shown to be the result of the process of the random and brutal nature of natural selection. Once an alternative explanation was recognized, both in the academic and popular mind, the power of a logical proof for the existence of God was unconvincing. The edifice of the logical proof of the design argument was reduced to rubble.

The late 20th century, however, has seen a remarkable re-emergence of design. I am not speaking here necessarily of the emergence of intelligent design which has in large part flowed out the creationist controversies in the US.[207] This has concentrated on the emergence of irreducible complexity in biological evolution and argued that God is the only answer. This has tended towards a 'god of the gaps' approach. If science does not have the answer then the temptation is to insert God as the answer to the scientific question. The trouble is that if then science comes along and fills in the 'gap', God is pushed out of the gap into irrelevancy. A similar temptation has been seen in those who have argued that if the Universe came through a Big Bang then 'who lit the blue touch paper'. Noting that our current scientific theories of general relativity and quantum theory are unable to describe the first 10^{-43} second of the Universe's history, some have suggested that this is where God comes in. The danger of this sort of approach is that someone such as Stephen Hawking comes along with a possible theory of quantum gravity which explains how the blue touch paper lights itself.[208]

While the movement of intelligent design has attracted a great deal of media interest, more remarkable is the revival of the design argument amongst physicists, many of whom have no religious axe to grind. There certainly have been Christians who have used their science to point to the existence of a Creator God, such as the physicist John Polkinghorne and the Director of the Human Genome Project Francis Collins.[209] But there have also been others such as Paul Davies who have argued that science pushes us to see an intelligence within or behind the Universe.[210]

Why should this be, given the intellectual heritage of Darwin's destruction of the design argument? The answer seems to be that the science of the origin and structure of the Universe pushes the religious questions. In particular, physicists are fascinated by a number of remarkable features of the Universe.

Anthropic balances

In the last few decades we have discovered that the laws and circumstances of the Universe need to be just right in order to give us a Universe of structure and intelligent self-conscious life. In his book *Just Six Numbers* the distinguished cosmologist Martin Rees notes the extraordinary fine tuning of six numbers fundamental to the Universe.[211] These numbers represent the ratio of the electric force to the gravitational force; how firmly atomic nuclei bind together; the amount of material in the Universe; the cosmological constant; the ratio of energy needed to disperse an object compared to its total rest mass energy; and the number of spatial dimensions in the Universe. If any of these numbers were only slightly different to what they are we would not be here.

Rees then sees three possible explanations. The first is simply to say that this is just the way things are. He finds this unsatisfying because the fine-tuning of these numbers is so remarkable that it poses why questions. The second is to see this fine-tuning as evidence of a Creator God, something that Polkinghorne and Collins would argue. His own answer is that the anthropic principle selects this Universe out of many. That is we see this fine-tuning because we are here. In other universes where these numbers were different there would be no one there to see them.

There are of course many theories of many universes. A couple of decades ago it was popular to believe that there was enough mass in the Universe to halt its expansion, leading to a contraction and then a big crunch. Some physicists went further and postulated that the Universe would then bounce into another Big Bang and one would then have an infinite series of oscillating universes. However, in 1999 it was discovered through observation of distant supernovae that the Universe was not slowing down in its expansion but accelerating destined to expand forever.

Another scenario came from Hugh Everett's interpretation of how the uncertainty of the quantum world collapsed into the certainty of the everyday world. Everett suggested that each quantum possibility was fulfilled by the Universe splitting into different universes leading to billions upon billions upon billions of parallel universes. The final scenario is that our Universe is one of many bubble universes undergoing expansion from an original quantum field. Now the crucial point in all of this is whether other Universe speculation is metaphysics or physics. Can we know that they are there by the passing of information from one Universe to another, or do we accept their existence on the basis of the prediction of theories which solve other problems to do with our early Universe? There is considerable disagreement on these matters at the moment. In any case, current speculation about the existence of other universes cautions us against resurrecting the proof of design argument. As long as we lack of physical evidence for other universes, it remains metaphysical speculation, and an alternative explanation to that of a Creator God.

Anthropic balances do not prove the existence of a Creator, but they do provoke questions and for some are pointers to the existence of a Creator. Sir Fred Hoyle, when he calculated the fine-tuning which makes possible the creation of carbon in the nuclear furnaces of stars, said, 'Nothing has shaken my atheism as much as this discovery'.

An intelligible order

Of course, these anthropic balances are not excuses for 'god of the gaps'. Many of these balances can and may have scientific explanations. But that does not make them any less extraordinary. Why is it that the Universe has such laws which make possible the development of self-conscious life? In contrast to the intelligent design movement, Polkinghorne and Collins are eager to find out how these balances can be explained scientifically, but this does not take away from the fact that it is an amazing feature of this Universe.

In the same way, other physicists find the beauty, simplicity, universality and intelligibility of the laws of physics themselves to be pointers to this Universe being creation. As Einstein once commented, 'the most incomprehensible thing about the Universe is that it is comprehensible.' Why are these amazing and often exotic laws intelligible to us? Some see some kind of rationality behind the Universe. Some Christians actually responded positively to Darwin's natural selection, with awe that God should have used an intricate process of biological laws, rather than the special design of each creature. Indeed this has a long tradition stretching back to Isaac Newton, who saw the laws of the Universe as work of the divine lawgiver. Johannes Kepler was 'carried away by unutterable rapture' as the correlation between orbital periods and mean diameters, which showed that the planets moved in elliptical orbits, was disclosed. The same can be said of some physicists today who see the laws of physics as a reflection of the consistent work of God in sustaining the Universe (see Chapter 15 by John Hedley Brooke).

An awe-inspiring Universe

The question of awe applies both at the popular and scientific level. In the popular mind, dramatic photographs of the Universe taken by the

Hubble Space Telescope engender a sense of the finite nature of human beings in such a vast Universe. This sense of awe has often led into worship. For example the Psalmist exclaims, 'The heavens declare the glory of God' (Psalm 19:1). This can sometimes be awe at ignorance, but is often an awe which is expanded by the insights of modern scientific knowledge.

A number of physicists also get this sense of awe in their work. Of course most of science is mundane, boring, pressured and beset with failure, but there are moments when the beauty of the scientific Universe or the fact that underneath the complexity of the Universe are a few elegant laws lead to what John Habgood, a former chemist and then Archbishop of York, called 'Woor lookatdat' moments. Indeed it can be argued that the design argument had power not because of the logical force of its argument but by its emotive power keying into people's awe at the Universe. The same thing seems to be happening today.

A revival of design?

The revival of the design argument in contemporary cosmology is a fascinating religious phenomenon. It could mean that physicists have never really read philosophy or understood the legacy of Darwin! Or maybe that the legacy of Darwin has pushed the question of design away from proofs and specific biological observations to the nature of the laws themselves.

This revival of design is characterized in three ways which are different from the classical design argument. First, it is more about questions than answers. The science seems to raise questions which point beyond science into philosophy, theology and religion. Second, it is more about pointers than proof. The design argument cannot be resurrected but it can be restated in terms of pointers towards a Creator God. Third, it is about emotive rather than explanatory force.

In considering the late 20th-century physics, an interesting parallel is found right back in the 19th-century England. In 1835, Temple Chevalier accepted the Chair of Mathematics at Durham University and also became Reader in Hebrew. He continued to hold both of these posts until 1871. In addition, in 1841 he became Professor of Astronomy and took the lead in establishing an observatory in Durham. He wrote many papers on astronomy and physics including meteorology, was the first to institute in England regular and continuous observation of sunspots, made important observations of Jupiter's moons, and the lunar crater Chevallier is named after him.

In 1826/7 he gave the Hulsean Lectures in Cambridge with the title 'On the proofs of Divine Power and Wisdom, derived from the study of astronomy and the evidence, doctrines and precepts of Revealed Religion'. These 20 sermons began following the structure of Psalm 19. This psalm begins reflecting on what can be known about God from the world, and then moves on to what can be known about God from his word, the scriptures. The first four sermons concentrated on his own interest in astronomy. Chevallier picks up themes of awe at the vastness of the Universe, the beauty of the scientific laws, and the specific circumstances that make life possible. Chevallier was not a creationist, nor was he into a God of the gaps. For him, science itself was a gift from God:

'In the heavens, as in every other part of creation, there exist proofs of power and design. And if we stop short in our researches, without extending our thoughts from the wonders of nature to the God of nature, we omit to do that which reason recommends and revelation enjoins'.

It is clear reading these sermons that what Chevallier meant by 'proofs' from astronomy were questions, pointers and an invitation to awe. From his basis of believing that God had revealed his existence and nature by becoming a human being in Jesus, Chevallier urges his readers to value science, and to see how it can point to the power and care of God. It is a tradition which continues in cosmology today, where a rich dialogue of science and belief is taking place. The legacy of Darwin has not been to close down that dialogue but perhaps to open it up into the bigger questions of creation of the Universe, human significance and scientific awe.

Epilogue: Science *and* religion, not science *or* religion

Michael O'Brien

As an anthropologist, I have built my career around understanding the evolution of humans, especially with respect to that decidedly human phenomenon termed 'culture'. Various approaches to understanding cultural evolution have been proposed, but the only one that has ever made much sense to me is Darwinian evolution. I use it as a framework on which to hang all aspects of the study of humans, from such traditional things as genes and teeth to more unconventional things such as language, kinship and tools. To me, those human features not directly controlled by genes are as subject to evolutionary processes such as natural selection and drift as bodily features are.

I not only practice anthropology, I teach it. As is common in most large anthropology departments in the US, faculty members in my department rotate the teaching of large sections of the introductory course. Unlike in the sciences and mathematical sciences, where introductory sections are taught in strict accordance with a course-wide syllabus, what to include or not to include in the individual sections of the basic anthropology course is at the discretion of the instructor. Given my intellectual bias, I teach the course from an evolutionary perspective.

I remember several years ago, somewhere around week seven of the course, a young woman in the middle of the auditorium raised her hand to ask a question during a lecture on natural selection. The question she asked ranks as probably the best I've ever had posed in any class. Helping to make it a great question was that it came from a freshman, whom we usually consider too naïve to ask great questions, and it came out of true puzzlement on her part. This is what she asked me: 'From the first day of class, you've woven every discussion around evolution, which, although I understand the arguments, I have some trouble with. But now I'm totally bewildered. On Sunday I saw you and your wife and kids at Mass, and, quite frankly, I was floored. You're obviously committed to evolution as an explanatory framework, but I'm supposing you also believe in God. But how can you believe in God *and* believe in evolution? I don't get that at all.'

This was one of those moments that makes you stop and think, but I pulled a response out of my head, answering simply, 'I don't believe in evolution.' This evoked a roomful of quizzical looks, but then I added something like, 'But neither do I believe that two and two equal four. Rather, I know two and two make four, just as I know that evolution provides a powerful means of explaining the natural world. Belief has absolutely nothing to do with it. On the other hand, do I know God exists? No; that's purely a matter of belief. But I don't spend a lot of time worrying about it one way or the other. I do worry, however, about building better evolutionary arguments about why nature, and that includes humans, looks the way it does. Importantly, those arguments have nothing to do with whether God exists. Don't make the fundamental mistake of confusing science and belief.'

But plenty of people *do* confuse the two. The current, and seemingly endless, debates over whether someone can be both a 'scientist' and a person who believes in God are not only tiring but intellectually dishonest. They cleverly conflate two of the three great sense-making systems – science and belief – that humans have devised in order to understand the world around them (common sense is the third). Perhaps 'conflation' is too soft a word because what we see most often is a complete polarization of science and belief. People tend to gravitate to one pole when they're scared of what others are offering. It is far easier, say, for scientists to place the blame for the sad state of science knowledge in America on Christian fundamentalists than it is to admit that perhaps they've helped create a polarization.

I share the concern of scientists that religion should be kept out of science, but I do not share the general paranoia exhibited by Richard Dawkins, Dan Dennett and others that theists are hiding under every bush, ready to hijack the science curricula in all 50 states. Living in America's heartland, I know all too well that people are for the most part underinformed about science, but I do not see them as rabid creationists, ready to replace test tubes with crucifixes and lab manuals with bibles. There are, to be sure, 'intelligent designers' out there who would love nothing more than to replace science with a design-based curriculum in the schools, but they are a minority. Of much greater significance are the millions of people who simply want the natural world explained to them in terms they can understand. It is far easier, though, to tell them that by definition if one believes in God, he or she cannot possibly be an evolutionist.

When we parade around publicly spouting jargon such as 'life results from the non-random survival of randomly varying replicators' – a T-shirt slogan that Dawkins once proposed – we are not going to attract many followers. But then again, if we are not that interested in followers, and more interested in showing how intelligent we are, then such mind-numbing slogans work just fine. This is unfortunate because what we could be demonstrating is that science can play an important role in helping us to understand how and why we construct beliefs. It does not play a role in determining the validity of beliefs, nor is it designed to. Rather, its analytical focus lies in the chemical-physical and cultural basis that underlies beliefs.

Dennett once characterized Darwin's ideas as 'dangerous', but contrary to how he and others might see it, those ideas are in no sense dangerous to either religion or belief systems. In fact, they are dangerous only to the outmoded notion made popular by Jean-Baptiste Lamarck that evolution is somehow guided by an organism's need for a certain feature in order to survive. Darwin quite nicely showed that in nature the production of variation is not guided by some need, nor does it require the existence of some invisible hand. Darwin's ideas are the basis of modern evolutionary theory. As such, they belong squarely in the realm of science. But do not conflate science as a sense-making system with belief as a sense-making system. They are both valid systems, and they are not exclusionary. I'm reminded of what Matthew (22:21) says: 'Render unto Caesar the things which are Caesar's, and unto God the things that are God's.'

Notes

1. J.D. Miller, E.C. Scott and S. Okamoto (2006) 'Public acceptance of evolution', in *Science* 313: 765–766.
2. M. Bywater (2008) 'Idiots are people too,' in *The Daily Telegraph*, 26 January 2008.
3. W. Nelson and T. Pipkin, *The Tao of Willie: A Guide to the Happiness in Your Heart* (New York: Gotham Press, 2007).
4. M. Earls, *The Herd* (Hoboken, NJ: John Wiley & Sons, 2007).
5. D.S. Whitley (2008), 'Religion,' in *Handbook of Archaeological Theories*, edited by R.A. Bentley, H.D.G. Maschner and C. Chippendale (Lanham, MD: AltaMira), pp. 547–566.
6. As discussed throughout this book, but see Gordy Slack's *The Battle Over the Meaning of Everything* (San Francisco: Jossey-Bass, 2007) for an engaging account of a court case over creationism in school, pitting parents against a Pennsylvania school board.
7. F. Fitzgerald (2007) 'Come one, come all,' in *The New Yorker,* 3 December 2007: 46–56.
8. See D. Martin, *On Secularization: Towards a Revised General Theory* (Aldershot: Ashgate, 2005).
9. R.I.M Dunbar and S. Shultz (2007) 'Evolution in the social brain', in *Science* 317: 1344–1347.
10. On evolutionary differences between copied and selected behaviours, see R.A. Bentley (2007) 'Fashion versus reason – then and now', in *Antiquity* 81: 1071–1073.
11. J. A. Coyne (2006) 'Cause of reason,' in *Times Literary Supplement*, 31 March 2006.
12. J. Diamond, *Guns, Germs and Steel* (London: Jonathan Cape, 1997).
13. L. Bergreen, *Marco Polo* (New York: Knopf, 2007), pp. 34 and 67.
14. G. Hart, *A Dictionary of Egyptian Gods and Goddesses* (London: Routledge, 1986).
15. See, for example, *Religion, Anthropology, and Cognitive Science*, edited by H. Whitehouse and J. Laidlaw (Durham, North Carolina: Carolina Academic, 2007).

16. See S.J. Shennan's *Genes, Memes and Human History* (London: Thames and Hudson, 2002).
17. L. Cronk, *That Complex Whole: Culture and the Evolution of Human Behavior* (Boulder, CO: Westview Press, 1999).
18. R.I.M. Dunbar and S. Shultz (2007) 'Evolution in the social brain', in *Science* 317: 1344–1347.
19. *Science, Evolution, and Creationism* is available online from National Academies of Science and Medicine (www.nationalacademies.org).
20. K.R. Miller, *Finding Darwin's God: A Scientist's Search for Common Ground Between God and Evolution* (New York: Harper Perennial, revised 2007).
21. J. Henrich and N. Henrich, *Why Humans Cooperate: A Cultural and Evolutionary Explanation* (Oxford: Oxford University Press, 2007).
22. R.D. Sommerfeld, H.-J. Krambeck, D. Semmann and M. Milinski (2007) 'Gossip as an alternative for direct observation in games of indirect reciprocity', in *Proceedings of the National Academy of Sciences* 104: 17435–17440.
23. See, for example, R.A. Bentley, M.W. Hahn and S. J. Shennan (2004) 'Random drift and culture change', in *Proceedings of the Royal Society B* 271: 1443–1450.
24. J.A. Coyne (2006) 'Cause of reason,' in *Times Literary Supplement*, 31 March 2006.
25. F. Gil-White (2001) 'Are ethnic groups biological "species" to the human brain?', in *Current Anthropology* 42: 515–554.
26. R. Pape, *Dying to Win: The Strategic Logic of Suicide Terrorism* (New York: Random House, 2005).
27. See, for example, S. Atran and A. Norenzayan (2004) 'Religion's evolutionary landscape', in *Behavioral and Brain Sciences* 27: 713–770.
28. M. Kaku, *Parallel Worlds* (New York: Penguin Books, 2005), p. 349.
29. See also K.R. Miller, *Finding Darwin's God* (New York: Harper Perennial, revised 2007).
30. See G. Miller (2007) 'The promise of parallel universes', in *Science* 317: 1341–1343.
31. See 'Glitch!', in *New Scientist*, 07 June 2003.
32. M. Kaku, discussing the theories of Alan Guth in *Parallel Worlds* (New York: Penguin Books, 2005), p. 328.

33. See J. Garreau, *Radical Evolution* (New York: Broadway Books, 2005).
34. J. Garreau, *Radical Evolution* (New York: Broadway Books, 2005), pp. 128–129.
35. Gordy Slack (1997) 'When science and religion collide or why Einstein wasn't an atheist,' *Mother Jones*, November/December 1997.
36. www.faraday-institute.org accessed 12/2/2008.
37. See J.H. Brooke *Science & Religion – Some Historical Perspectives* (Cambridge: Cambridge University Press, 1991): and also D.C. Lindberg and R. Numbers, *When Science and Christianity Meet* (Chicago: University of Chicago Press, 2004).
38. S. Shapin, *The Scientific Revolution* (Chicago: University of Chicago Press, 1996).
39. S. Harris, *Letter to a Christian Nation* (London: Bantam Press, 2007); R. Dawkins, *The God Delusion* (London: Bantam Press, 2006); C. Hitchens, *God Is Not Great: The Case Against Religion* (London: Atlantic Books, 2007).
40. C.A. Russell (1989) 'The conflict metaphor and its social origins,' in *Science and Christian Belief* 1: 3–26.
41. M. Stenmark, *How to Relate Science and Religion* (Michigan: Eerdmans, 2004).
42. For a brief introduction, see D.R. Alexander, (2007) 'Models for relating science and religion' (Faraday Paper No 3), available at: www.stedmunds.cam.ac.uk/faraday/Papers.php accessed 12/2/2008.
43. S.J. Gould, *Rock of Ages* (New York: Ballantine Books, 2002).
44. Augustine, *Literal Commentary on Genesis*, (AD 415): 'When such a thing happens, it appears to us as an event contrary to nature. But with God it is not so; for him "nature" is what he does.'
45. For example, see: the Science and Religion in Schools Project at http://www.srsp.net.
46. http://www.st-edmunds.cam.ac.uk/faraday/Courses.php accessed 12/2/2008.
47. http://www.templeton-cambridge.org/ accessed 12/2/2008.
48. On fuzzy sets and religion, see B. Wilson (1998), 'From the lexical to the polythetic: a brief history of the definition of religion,' in *What is*

Religion? Origins, Definitions, and Explanations, edited by B. Wilson and T. Idinopolus (Leiden: Brill), pp. 142–162.

49. S. Harris, *The End of Faith* (New York: Norton, 2005) and *Letter to a Christian Nation* (New York: Knopf, 2006).
50. Granted, there are enough ambiguities that creep into Harris's arguments, plus enough additional complications that arise if we include kindred works such as Daniel Dennett's *Breaking the Spell: Religion as a Natural Phenomenon* (New York: Viking, 2006), that sweeping generalizations are somewhat risky. Nevertheless it is useful to treat Harris as a representative new atheist and focus on his central arguments.
51. S. Harris, *Letter to a Christian Nation* (New York: Knopf, 2006), pp. 9, 4.
52. S. Harris, *Letter to a Christian Nation* , pp. 9, 7 and 5.
53. S. Harris, *End of Faith* (New York: Norton, 2005), pp. 68 and 21.
54. Obviously I have not chosen to ignore Harris, but I do propose to bracket two aspects of his work. One is how he conflates conservative Christianity with a monolithic reading of Islam. Another is his overlap with mainstream US punditry about Middle Eastern conflicts—for example, his vision of 'Islamo-fascism,' apologetics for the use of torture, and failure to judge Israeli religious-political behaviors by the same standards used for Christians and muslims.
55. Ralph Norman and John Bohstedt, personal communications, quoted by permission.
56. Readers will have to explore this issue case by case. For more, see M. Hulsether (2004) 'New approaches to the study of religion and culture,' in *New Approaches to the Study of Religion*, edited by Peter Antes, et al. (Verlag de Gruyter), pp. 344–382.
57. Björk, 'I See You Who Are,' *Volta* (New York: Atlantic Recording Company, 2007).
58. S. Harris, *The End of Faith* , p. 221.
59. S. Harris, 'The Sacrifice of Reason,' http://newsweek.washingtonpost.com/onfaith, accessed 9/2/2007.
60. S. Harris, *Letter to a Christian Nation*, p. 54.
61. K. Armstrong (2006), 'Is immortality important?' *Harvard Divinity Bulletin* 34: 20–21.

62. G. Wolf (2006) 'The crusade against religion,' in *Wired News*, 23 October 2006.
63. S. Harris, *The End of Faith*, p. 293.
64. S. Harris, *The End of Faith* , p. 215.
65. S. Harris, *The End of Faith,* p. 221.
66. S. Harris, *The End of Faith* , p. 223.
67. T. Trautmann (1992) 'The revolution in ethnological time', in *Man* 27: 379–397.
68. R. Dawkins, *The Selfish Gene* (Oxford: Oxford University Press, 1976), pp. 47 and 92.
69. D.H. Durham, *Co-Evolution: Genes, Culture and Human Diversity* (Stanford: Stanford University Press, 1991).
70. M. Sahlins, *Islands of History* (Chicago: Chicago University Press, 1985), p. 9.
71. E.A. Povinalli (1993) '"Might be something": The language of indeterminacy in Australian Aboriginal land use', in *Man* 28: 679–704.
72. See, for example, G.M. Wightman, D.M. Jackson, and L.V.L. Williams (1991) *Alawa Ethnobotany: Aboriginal Plant Use from Minyerri, Northern Australia*. (Darwin: Conservation Commission of the Northern Territory,) or see L. Baker, S. Woenne-Green and the Mutitjulu Community (1993)'Anangu knowledge of vertebrates and the environment' in *Uluru Fauna*, edited by N.T.J. Reid, J. Kerle and S. Morton (Canberra: Australian National Parks and Wildlife Service), pp. 79–132.
73. R.A. Gould (1971) 'The archaeologist as ethnographer: A case from the Western Desert of Australia', in *World Archaeology* 3: 143–177.
74. F. Myers (1986) 'Always ask: resource use and land ownership among Pintupi Aborigines of the Australian Western Desert,' in *Resource Managers: North American and Australian Hunter-Gatherers*, edited by N. Williams and E. Hunn (Australian Institute of Aboriginal Studies), pp. 173–195. Also see R. Layton (1989) 'Are social anthropology and sociobiology compatible?', in *The Comparative Socio-Ecology of Mammals and Man*, edited by R. Foley and V. Standen (Oxford: Blackwell), pp. 433–455.

    For maps and diagrams of Alawa country see R.L. Layton (1997), 'Representing and translating people's place in the landscape of northern Australia' in After Writing Culture, edited by A. James,

J. Hockey and A. Dawson (London: Routledge), pp. 122–143, and R. Layton (1999) 'The Alawa totemic landscape: economy, religion and politics' in The Archaeology and Anthropology of Landscape, edited by P. Ucko and R. Layton (London: Routledge), pp. 219–239.

75. R.A. Eve and F.B. Harrold *The Creationist Movement in Modern America* (Boston: Twayne, 1991).
76. T. Rowse (1988) 'Middle Australia and the noble savage: a political romance', in *Past and Present: the Construction of Aboriginality,* edited by J. Beckett (Canberra: Aboriginal Studies Press, 1998) pp. 170 and 175.
77. F. Harrold, R. Eve and J. Taylor (2004) 'Creationism, American-style', in *The Cultures of Creationism,* edited by L. Carlin and S. Coleman (Ashgate), pp. 67–84.
78. J. Barker (2004) 'Creationism in Canada', in *The Cultures of Creationism,* edited by L. Carlin and S. Coleman (Aldershot: Ashgate), pp. 85–108.
79. S. Coleman and L. Carlin, editors, *The Cultures of Creationism* (Aldershot: Ashgate, 2004).
80. S. Crown (2006) 'Why Creationism is wrong,' in *The Guardian,* 29 May 2006.
81. A. McGrath, *Dawkins' God: Genes, Memes, and the Meaning of Life* (Massachusetts: Blackwell, 2004).
82. See R. Dawkins, *River Out of Eden* (New York: Basic Books, 1995), p. 33. And also R. Dawkins, *A Devil's Chaplain* (London: Phoenix, 2004), pp. 18 and 137.
83. R. Dawkins, *A Devil's Chaplain* (London: Phoenix, 2004), p. 178.
84. See E. Gellner, *Postmodernism, Reason and Religion* (London: Routledge, 1992).
85. R. Dawkins, *A Devil's Chaplain* (London: Phoenix, 2004), p. 31.
86. E.g. R. H Gundry, *Jesus the Word According to John the Sectarian* (Grand Rapids: Eerdmans, 2001).
87. K. Poewe (1994) 'Rethinking the relationship of anthropology to science and religion,' in *Charismatic Christianity as a Global Culture*, edited by K. Poewe (Columbia: University of South Carolina Press), pp. 234–58.
88. R. Dawkins, *A Devil's Chaplain* (London: Phoenix, 2004), p. 185.
89. See R. Wrangham and D. Peterson *Demonic Males: Apes and the Origins of Human Violence* (Boston: Houghton Mifflin, 1996), Chapter 1.

90. See Michael Shermer's *eSkeptic* newsletter (www.skeptic.com), 8 August 2007.
91. We must remember that evidence for violence is often evidence for warfare, but a lack of evidence for violence is never evidence for a lack of warfare! Archaeologists have yet to come up with an archaeological signature for peace, but a lack of evidence for violence is not such a measure.
92. See William Calvin's *The Ascent of Mind* (london: Bantam, 1990), Chapter 8.
93. See T.D. White (1985) 'Cut marks on the Bodo cranium: A case of prehistoric defleshing', in *American Journal of Physical Anthropology* 69: 503–509.
94. F. Wendorf (1968) 'Site 117: A Nubian Paleolithic graveyard near Jebel Sahara, Sudan' in *The Prehistory of Nubia, vol. 2,* edited by F. Wendorf (Dallas: Southern Methodist University Press), pp. 954–995.
95. See D.L. Martin and D.W. Frayer, *Troubled Times: Violence and Warfare in the Past* (Amsterdam: Gordon and Breach, 1997), pp. 181–216.
96. See F.J. Melbye and S.I. Fairgrieve SI (1994) 'A massacre and possible cannibalism in the Canadian Arctic', in *Arctic Anthropology* 31: 57–77; also K.L. Reedy-Maschner and H.D.G. Maschner (1999) 'Marauding middlemen: Western expansion and violent conflict in the Subarctic', in *Ethnohistory* 46: 703–743.
97. M. Mann, *The Dark Side of Democracy* (Cambridge: Cambridge University Press, 2004).
98. Such as R.B. Ferguson and N.L. Whitehead, *War in the Tribal Zone* (Santa fe, New Mexico: School of American Research Press, 1992), p. 38.
99. F. Gil-White (2001) 'Are ethnic groups biological "species" to the human brain?', in *Current Anthropology* 42: 515–554.
100. See H.D.G. Maschner and K.L. Reedy-Maschner (1998) 'Raid, retreat, defend (repeat): The archaeology and ethnohistory of warfare on the North Pacific Rim', in *Journal of Anthropological Archaeology* 17: 19–51.
101. Or even profit from them – see D. Farah and S. Braun, *Merchant of Death* (New Jersey: Wiley, 2007).
102. See H. Sides, *Blood and Thunder: An Epic of the American West* (New York: Doubleday, 2006), and also T. Roberts, *Frontier Justice: A History of*

the Gulf Country to 1900 (Queensland: University of Queensland Press, 2006).

103. G. Dipellegrino, L. Fadiga, L. Fogassi, V. Gallese and G. Rizzolatti (1992) 'Understanding motor events – a neurophysiological study', in *Experimental Brain Research* 91: 176–180.
104. See R. Mukamel, A.D. Ekstrom, J.T. Kaplan M. Iacoboni and I. Fried (2007) 'Mirror properties of single cells in human medial frontal cortex', presented at the Society for Neuroscience meeting on November 4, 2007.
105. See Steven Mithen's *Prehistory of the Mind* (Cambridge: Cambridge University Press, 1996).
106. See V.S. Ramachandran (2000) 'Mirror neurons and imitation learning as the driving force behind "the great leap forward" in human evolution,' in *The Edge* (www.edge.org) 29 May 2000.
107. See note 104.
108. L. Wolpert, *Six Impossible Things Before Breakfast* (London: Faber, 2006).
109. See A.M. Leslie (1995) 'A theory of agency', in *Causal Cognition*, edited by D. Sperber, D. Premak and A.J. Premak (Oxford: Clarendon Press, 1995) pp. 121–142.
110. See R. Corrigan and P. Denton (1996) 'Causal understanding as a developmental primitive', in *Developmental Review* 16: 162–202; or See A. Schlottmann et al. (2002). 'Children's intuitions of perceptual causality', in *Child Development* 73: 1656–1677.
111. M. Tomasello, *The Cultural Origins of Human Cognition* (Cambridge: Harvard University Press, 1999).
112. D.J. Povinelli, *Folk Physics for Apes* (Oxford: Oxford University Press, 2000).
113. M. Hauser, *Wild Minds* (London: Allen Lane, 2000).
114. See J. Chappell and A. Kacelnik (2002) 'Tool selectivity in a non-primate, the New Caledonian crow (Corvus moneduloides)" in *Animal Cognition* 5: 71–78.
115. K. Oakley, *Man the Tool-Maker* (London: British Museum Press, 1949).
116. See S.H. Johnson-Frey (2004) 'The neural basis of complex tool use in humans', in *Trends in Cognitive Sciences* 8: 71–78 (Johnson-Frey, 2004).

117. See S.H. Ambrose (2001) 'Paleolithic technology and human evolution', in *Science* 291: 1748–1752.
118. R. Dunbar, *The Human Story* (London: Faber, 2004).
119. See also L. Wolpert, (2003) 'Causal belief and the origin of technology', in *Philosophical Transactions of the Royal Society A* 361: 1709–1719.
120. H.G. Koenig, M.E. Mccullough and D.B. Larson,. *Handbook of Religion and Health* (Oxford: Oxford University Press, 2001).
121. P. Boyer, *Religion Explained* (New York: Basic Books, 2001).
122. See R.R. Griffiths, W.A. Richards, U. McCann and R. Jesse . (2006) 'Psilo-cybin can occasion mystical-type experiences having substantial and sustained personal meaning and spiritual significance', in *Psycho-pharmacology* 187: 268–283.
123. D.S. Wilson, *Darwin's Cathedral* (Chicago: University of Chicago Press, 2002).
124. P. Boyer, *Religion Explained* (New York: Basic Books, 2002).
125. L. Wolpert, *Six Impossible Things Before Breakfast* (London: Faber, 2006).
126. D. Dennett *Breaking the Spell: Religion as a Natural Phenomenon* (New Jersey: Penguin, 2007).
127. P. Boyer, *Religion Explained* (New York: Basic Books, 2002).
128. H. Whitehouse, *Modes of Religiosity: A Cognitive Theory of Cultural Transmission* (Lanham, MD : AltaMira, 2004).
129. C. Renfrew, (editor) *The Archaeology of Cult: The Sanctuary at Phylakopi* (London: Thames and Hudson, 1985).
130. For a review of the evidence, see R. Gargett (1989) 'Grave shortcomings: the evidence for Neanderthal burial', in *Current Anthropology* 30: 157–190.
131. See C.S. Henshilwood et al. (2002) 'Emergence of modern behaviour: Middle Stone Age engravings from South Africa', in *Science* 295: 1278–1279. Also see F.D Errico, C. Henshilwood, M. Vanhaeren and K. van Niekerk (2005) '*Nassarius kraussianus* shell beads from Blombos Cave: evidence for symbolic behaviour in the Middle Stone Age', in *Journal of Human Evolution* 48: 3–24.

132. B. Finlayson and S.J. Mithen (editors). *The Early Prehistory of Wadi Faynan, Southern Jordan* (Oxford Books, 2007).
133. S.J. Mithen, B. Finlayson and R. Shaffrey (2005) 'Sexual symbolism in the Early Neolithic of the southern Levant: pestles and mortars from WF16' in *Documenta Prehistorica* 32: 103–110.
134. S.J. Mithen, K. Wicks and J. Hill (2007) 'Fiskary Bay: A Mesolithic fishing camp on Coll', in *Scottish Archaeology News* 55: 14–15.
135. S.J. Mithen (editor). *Hunter-Gatherer Landscape Archaeology: The Southern Hebrides Mesolithic Project 1988–1998* (McDonald Institute, 2000).
136. See S.J. Mithen, The Prehistory of the Mind (London & New York: Thames & Hudson, 1996), and also S.J. Mithen, The Singing Neanderthals: The Origins of Music, Language, Mind and Body (London: Weidenfeld & Nicolson, 2005).
137. C.W. Marean, M. Bar-Matthews, J. Bernatchez, E. Fisher, P. Goldberg, A.I.R. Herries, Z. Jacobs, A. Jerardino, P. Karkanas, T. Minichillo, P.J. Nilssen, E. Thompson, I. Watts and H.M. Williams (2007) 'Early human use of marine resources and pigment in South Africa during the Middle Pleistocene', in *Nature* 449: 905–908.
138. See S.J. Mithen, *The Singing Neanderthals*, chapter entitled 'Neanderthals in Love'.
139. F. D'Errico and A. Nowell (2000) 'A new look at the Berekhat Ram figurine: Implications for the origins of symbolism', in *Cambridge Archaeological Journal* 10: 123–67.
140. S. J. Mithen (1998) 'The supernatural beings of prehistory: the external symbolic storage of religious ideas' in *Cognition and Culture: The Archaeology of Symbolic Storage*, edited by C. Scarre and C. Renfrew (McDonald Institute), pp. 97–106.
141. M. Day (2004) 'Religion, off-line cognition and the extended mind', in *Journal of Cognition and Culture* 4: 101–121 (see p. 116).
142. For discussion of language evolution see S.J. Mithen, *The Singing Neanderthals*.
143. M. Houellebecq, *La possibilité d'une île* (Paris: Fayard, 2005); translation here by Sarah Wright.

144. W. Jamieson, *Father Knows Less or 'Can I Cook My Sister?': One Dad's Quest to Answer His Son's Most Baffling Questions* (New York: Putnam, 2007).
145. As I am quoted in W. Jamieson's *Father Knows Less or "Can I Cook My Sister?": One Dad's Quest to Answer His Son's Most Baffling Questions* (New York: Putnam, 2007), pp. 246ff.
146. See the Delgado and Paez transcripts in *Cannibal: The History of the People Eaters*, edited by D. Korn, M. Radice and C. Hawes (Channel 4 Books, 2001) p. 116.
147. See T. Taylor, *The Buried Soul: How Humans Invented Death* (London: Fourth Estate, 2002), p. 74.
148. See 'The Tradescant Collection' on the Ashmolean Museum website (www.ashmolean.org).
149. W. Paley, *Natural Theology* (Oxford: Oxford University Press, 2006 edition).
150. R. Dawkins, *The Blind Watchmaker* (New York: Norton, 1986).
151. See www.tdctrade.com , December 1999.
152. J.-P. Sartre, *Critique of Dialectical Reason* (London: Verso Books edition, 2004).
153. D.L. Clarke, *Analytical Archaeology* (New York: Columbia University Press, 1978).
154. See, for example, the Foreward by Mary Midgley, as well as her book, *The Myths We Live By* (London: Routledge, 2003).
155. For a review, see T. Taylor (2008) 'Materiality' in *Handbook of Archaeological Theories* edited by R.A. Bentley, H.D.G. Maschner and C. Chippindale (Lanham, MD: AltaMira Press), pp. 297–320.
156. C. Geertz, *The Interpretation of Cultures* (London: Fontana Press, new edition, 1993).
157. A.B. Newberg and M.R. Waldman, *Born to Believe: God, Science and the Origin of Ordinary and Extraodinary Beliefs* (New York: Free Press, 2007).
158. A.B. Newberg, E.G. d'Aquili and V. Rouse (2001). Why God Won't Go Away: Brain Science and the Biology of Belief. New York: Ballentine.
159. Reprinted with permission from *The Skeptic* (www.skeptic.com) 4 July 2007.

160. D.S. Wilson, *Darwin's Cathedral: Evolution, Religion, and the Nature of Society* (Chicago: University of Chicago Press, 2003).
161. R. Dawkins, *The God Delusion* (New York: Houghton Mifflin, 2006).
162. G. C. Williams, *Adaptation and Natural Selection* (Princeton: Princeton University Press, 1966).
163. See R. Dawkins, *The Selfish Gene: 30th Anniversary Edition* (Oxford: Oxford University Press, 2006).
164. R. Dawkins, *The Extended Phenotype: The Long Reach of the Gene* (Oxford: Oxford University Press, 1982), p. 6.
165. B. Kerr, C. Neuhauser, B. J. M. Bohannan and A. M. Dean (2006) 'Local migration promotes competitive restraint in a host–pathogen tragedy of the commons', in *Nature* 442: 75–78.
166. D.S. Wilson and E.O. Wilson (2007), 'Rethinking the theoretical foundation of sociobiology', in *Quarterly Review of Biology* 82: 327–348. For similar views in psychology, see also J. Haidt (2007) 'The new synthesis in moral psychology' in *Science* 316: 998–1002.
167. L. Margulis, *Origin of Eukaryotic Cells* (New Haven, CT: Yale University Press, 1970).
168. P. Richerson and R. Boyd, *Not By Genes Alone: How Culture Transformed Human Evolution* (Chicago: University of Chicago Press, 2005).
169. R. Dawkins *The God Delusion* (London: Bantam Press, 2006), pp. 167–168.
170. M. Csikszentmihalyi, *Flow* (New York: Harper and Collins, 1991) and *The Evolving Self* (New York: Harper, 1994).
171. D.S. Wilson and M. Csikszentmihalyi (2006) 'Health and the Ecology of Altruism,' in *The Science of Altruism and Health*, edited by S.G. Post (Oxford: Oxford University Press, 2006), Chapter 17.
172. R. Dawkins, *The God Delusion* (London: Bantam Press, 2006); C. Hitchens, *God is Not Great* (Atlantic Books, 2007); S. Harris, *The End of Faith* (London: Free Press, 2005).
173. K. Ward, *Is Religion Dangerous?* (London: Lion, 2007); C. Kimball *When Religion Becomes Evil* (San Francisco: HarperSanFrancisco, 2002).
174. C. Hitchens, *God is Not Great* (Atlantic Books, 2007), p. 190.
175. C. Hitchens, *God is Not Great*, p. 205.

176. R. Dawkins, *The God Delusion* (London: Bantam Press, 2006), p. 37.
177. C. Kimball, *When Religion Becomes Evil* (San Francisco: Harper SanFrancisco, 2002), p. 41.
178. K. Ward, *Is Religion Dangerous?* (London: Lion, 2007), pp. 68–69.
179. For a full discussion of Aum's violence, see I. Reader, *Religious Violence in Contemporary Japan* (Honolulu: University of Hawaii Press, 2000).
180. See http://www.lancs.ac.uk/fass/religstudies/research/projects/burnley.htm
181. I. Reader *Religious Violence in Contemporary Japan* (Honolulu: University of Hawaii Press, 2000), pp. 28–31.
182. *Aggañña Sutta, Digha Nikaya* (Pāli Text Society, 1910).
183. The State Peace & Development Council, which changed its name from State Law & Order Restoration Council in 1997, has been in power since 1988.
184. When government troops tried to break up a peaceful rally in Pakokku, a group of monks was hurt. Angered by their aggression, the monks held officials hostage. When no apology was forthcoming from the government, they began protesting in numbers on the streets that spread to Yangon and other cities. They were, however, not calling for regime change initially, but for an apology for the mistreatment of monks.
185. There are 227 monastic rules and regulations stipulated for Buddhist monks in the Theravāda tradition.
186. *The Heritage of the Bhikkhu: A Short History of the Bhikkhu in the Educational, Cultural, Social, and Political Life* (New York: Grove Press. 1974).
187. *The Correspondence of Charles Darwin Vol. 7, 1858–1859* (Cambridge: Cambridge University Press, 1991), p. 375.
188. *The Correspondence of Charles Darwin Vol. 7, 1858–1859*, p. 432.
189. See, for example, A. Desmond and J. Moore, *Darwin: The Life of a Tormented Evolutionist* (New York: Norton, 1994), p. 122.
190. P. Harrison (2006) 'Miracles, early modern science, and rational religion', in *Church History* 75: 493–511.
191. C.F. Davis, *The Evidential Force of Religious Experience* (Oxford: Oxford University Press, 1999).

192. Frank Close, Interview reported in *The Daily Telegraph*, 3 November 1993.
193. Cited by T Söderqvist, 'Existential Projects and Existential Choice in Science: Science Biography as an Edifying Genre' in *Telling Lives in Science*, edited by M. Shortland and R. Yeo (Cambridge: Cambridge University Press, 1996), p. 65.
194. R. Dawkins, *Unweaving the Rainbow* (Mariner, 2000).
195. As in my chapter, 'Konzeptwandel nach dem Kontakt', in *Leben im All* edited by Tobias Daniel Wabbel (Patmos, Dusseldorf, 2005), pp. 127–140.
196. W. H. Calvin, *How the Shaman Stole the Moon* (London: Bantam Press, 1991). See at *WilliamCalvin.com/bk6.*
197. The same thing happens in modern medicine all the time. Unless you know the 'natural history of the disease' (all of those ups and downs even without treatment) you can't be sure your treatment was the cause of the patient getting better. Even if you can rule that out, getting better might merely have been your treatment's placebo effect.
198. Two Chinese astrologers, Hsi and Ho, had apparently failed to predict the eclipse of 22 October 2134 BC, and as a result were beheaded by an unhappy emperor.
199. W. H. Calvin (2003) 'Adam Zeman's *Consciousness: A User's Guide*,' in *New York Times* Book Review 28 September 2003: p. 24. See also http://WilliamCalvin.com/2003/consciousness.htm.
200. Frans de Waal (2004), 'How animals do business,' *Scientific American* 292(4): 72–79.
201. S. Brand (1990), 'Learning from the earthquake'. *Whole Earth Review* 68 (Fall, 1990).
202. See W. H. Calvin, *A Brief History of the Mind: From Apes to Intellect and Beyond*. (Oxford: Oxford University Press, 2004).
203. I. McDougall, F. H. Brown and J. G. Fleagle (2005) 'Stratigraphic placement and age of modern humans from Kibish, Ethiopia', in *Nature* 433: 733–736.
204. J. Pfeiffer, *The Creative Explosion* (New York: Harper and Row, 1982).

205. P. Ward and D. Brownlee, *Rare Earth* (New York: Copernicus, 2000).
206. S. Coleman and L. Carlin, editors *The Cultures of Creationism* (Aldershot: Ashgate, 2004); E. Lucas, *Can We Believe Genesis Today?* (Leicester: IVP, 2001).
207. B. Forrest and P. R. Goss, *Creationism's Trojan Horse: The Wedge of Intelligent Design* (Oxford: Oxford University Press, 2004).
208. D. Wilkinson, *God, Time and Stephen Hawking* (London: Monarch, 2001).
209. F. Collins, *The Language of God: A Scientist Presents Evidence for Belief* (New York: Simon and Schuster, 2006); J.C. Polkinghorne, *The Faith of a Physicist* (Princeton: Princeton University Press, 1994).
210. P. Davies *The Goldilocks Enigma: Why Is the Universe Just Right for Life?* (London: Penguin, 2007).
211. M. Rees, *Just Six Numbers: The Deep Forces that Shape the Universe* (London: Weidenfeld and Nicholson, 2000).

Index